Grammar

Titles in the Resource Books for Teachers series

Beginners
Peter Grundy

Classroom Dynamics
Jill Hadfield

Conversation
Rob Nolasco and Lois Arthur

Creative Poetry Writing
Jane Spiro

Cultural Awareness
Barry Tomalin and Susan Stempleski

Dictionaries
Jon Wright

Drama
Charlyn Wessels

Drama and Improvisation
Ken Wilson

English for Specific Purposes
Keith Harding

Exam Classes
Peter May

Film
Susan Stempleski and Barry Tomalin

Global Issues
Ricardo Sampedro and Susan Hillyard

Grammar
Scott Thornbury

Grammar Dictation
Ruth Wajnryb

Homework
Lesley Painter

The Internet
Scott Windeatt, David Hardisty, and D. Eastment

Learner-based Teaching
Colin Campbell and Hanna Kryszewska

Letters
Nicky Burbidge, Peta Gray, Sheila Levy, and Mario Rinvolucri

Listening
Goodith White

Literature
Alan Duff and Alan Maley

Music and Song
Tim Murphey

Newspapers
Peter Grundy

Project Work 2nd edition
Diana L. Fried-Booth

Pronunciation
Clement Laroy

Role Play
Gillian Porter Ladousse

Storybuilding
Jane Spiro

Teaching Other Subjects Through English
Sheelagh Deller and Chris Price

Teenagers
Gordon Lewis

Vocabulary 2nd edition
John Morgan and Mario Rinvolucri

Writing 2nd edition
Tricia Hedge

Primary Resource Books

Art and Crafts with Children
Andrew Wright

Assessing Young Learners
Sophie Ioannou-Georgiou and Pavlos Pavlou

Creating Chants and Songs
Carolyn Graham

Creating Stories with Children
Andrew Wright

Drama with Children
Sarah Phillips

Games for Children
Gordon Lewis with Günther Bedson

Grammar for Young Learners
Gordon Lewis and Hans Mol

The Internet and Young Learners
Gordon Lewis

Projects with Young Learners
Diane Phillips, Sarah Burwood, and Helen Dunford

Storytelling with Children
Andrew Wright

Very Young Learners
Vanessa Reilly and Sheila M. Ward

Writing with Children
Jackie Reilly and Vanessa Reilly

Young Learners
Sarah Phillips

Resource Books for Teachers
series editor Alan Maley

Grammar

Scott Thornbury

OXFORD
UNIVERSITY PRESS

OXFORD
UNIVERSITY PRESS

Great Clarendon Street, Oxford OX2 6DP

Oxford University Press is a department of the University of Oxford. It furthers the University's objective of excellence in research, scholarship, and education by publishing worldwide in

Oxford New York

Auckland Cape Town Dar es Salaam Hong Kong Karachi Kuala Lumpur Madrid Melbourne Mexico City Nairobi New Delhi Shanghai Taipei Toronto

With offices in

Argentina Austria Brazil Chile Czech Republic France Greece Guatemala Hungary Italy Japan Poland Portugal Singapore South Korea Switzerland Thailand Turkey Ukraine Vietnam

OXFORD and OXFORD ENGLISH are registered trade marks of Oxford University Press in the UK and in certain other countries

First published 2006
2015 2014 2013 2012
10 9 8 7 6 5

ISBN: 978 0 19 442192 8

Printed in Great Britain by Clays Ltd, St Ives plc

Acknowledgements

The authors and publisher are grateful to the following for permission to reprint copyright material:

John Agard c/o Caroline Sheldon Literary Agency Limited for permission to reprint the poem 'Don't Call Alligator Long Mouth Till You Cross The River' from *Say It Again Granny* by John Agard (Bodley Head, 1986), copyright © John Agard 1986.

Amots Dafni and Springer-Verlag GmbH for an extract from 'The Role of Flower Inclination, Depth, and Height in the Preferences of a Pollinating Beetle (Coleoptera: Glaphyridae)', copyright © Amots Dafni 2004, first published in *Journal of Insect Behaviour* Vol.17/6 November 2004 (Springer-Verlag GmbH, 2004), reprinted by permission of the author and publisher.

Cambridge University Press and Mario Rinvolucri for permission to use the 'Grammar Auction' idea from *Grammar Games*, copyright © Mario Rinvolucri 1984, reprinted by permission of the author and publisher.

Cambridge University Press and Dave Willis for permission to use an idea from *Rules, Patterns and Words* (Cambridge University Press, 2003), copyright © Dave Willis 2003, reprinted by permission of the author and publisher.

City Explorer Enterprises Ltd. for an extract from *Explorer* magazine on 'Café Afrika' from issue 16, December 2003, reprinted by permission of the publisher.

G. Gerngross, H. Puchta, and J. Stranks for permission to use the idea for activity 2.24, originally published in *Creative Grammar Practice* (Helbling Languages, 2006).

Guardian Newspapers Limited for an extract abridged from the Patrick Marber column copyright © Guardian Newspapers Limited 1994, first published in *The Observer* 13.02.94, reprinted by permission of the publisher.

IPC Media Limited for extracts from 'Dinner disaster', 'Gone off the boil', and 'Pyjama palaver', all taken from issue no. 464: 26.02.03 of *Mizz* Magazine, copyright IPC Media Limited 2003, reprinted by permission of the publisher.

Kingfisher Books for extracts from 'Chameleon' from *Pocket Encyclopedia* by A. Jack (Kingfisher Books, 1983) and from 'Skeleton and Muscles' from *Visual Factfinder* (Kingfisher Books, 1993).

Macmillan Education for permission to reproduce the table 'I've never seen a kangaroo' from *Highlight Pre-Intermediate Student Book* by Scott Thornbury (Heinemann, 1994).
Luke Meddings for permission to use the ideas in Activity 2.22.

Miles Kelly Publishing Ltd for permission to reproduce extracts from *Great Little Encyclopedia*, copyright © Miles Kelly Publishing Limited 2003.

Oxford University Press Extract for permission to reproduce extracts from *www.oup.com/elt/global/teachersclub/teaching/debate/grammar* copyright © Oxford University Press, *Natural English Intermediate Listening Booklet* by Ruth Gairns and Stuart Williams (copyright © Oxford University Press 2002), *Natural Grammar* by Scott Thornbury (copyright © Oxford University Press, 2004), *Streamline English Departures* by Bernard Hartley and Peter Viney (Oxford University Press, 1978), copyright © Bernard Hartley and Peter Viney 1978, and *The Good Grammar Book* by Michael Swan and Catherine Walter (Oxford University Press, 2001), copyright © Michael Swan and Catherine Walter 2001; and for entries for 'own' taken from the *Oxford Advanced Learners Dictionary* 7th Edition (Oxford University Press, 2005).

Pearson Education Ltd. for permission to reproduce a table from *Building Strategies* by Brian Abbs et al (Longman, 1975).

Penguin Books Ltd. for a joke taken from *The Great Puffin Joke Directory* by Brough Girling (Puffin Books, 1990), text copyright © Brough Girling 1990.

Pantheon Books, a division of Random House Inc., for an extract from 'Monkey Learns to Weave' from *Arab Folk Tales* edited by Inea Bushnaq (Penguin, 1986), copyright © Inea Bushnaq 1986.

Random House Group Ltd. for permission to reprint the poem 'Walking At Dusk' from *Silence In The Snowy Fields And Other Poems* by Robert Bly (Jonathan Cape, 1967).

Sneak Magazine for an extract from 'Mind the gap!' taken from issue 82: 02.12.03, reprinted by permission of the publisher.

Ian Soper for permission to use the ideas in Activity 2.15.

Although we have tried to trace and contact copyright holders before publication, in some cases this has not been possible. If contacted we will be pleased to rectify any errors or omissions at the earliest opportunity.

Contents

The authors and series editor

Scott Thornbury is an experienced teacher, teacher trainer, and materials writer. Originally from New Zealand, he has taught English, and trained teachers of English, in Egypt, the UK, and Spain, where he now lives. Teacher education is his specialism, and was the subject of his MA dissertation at the University of Reading, UK. Through many organisations including (IATEFL, TESOL, APAC (Catalonia), FAAPI (Argentina), LAURELS, and APPI (Portugal), as well as through International House schools, he has been involved in many accredited teacher training schemes, both pre- service and in-service, and has met and talked to hundreds of teachers worldwide. He is the author of numerous articles and course books, as well as several books for teachers: *About Language*, *Uncovering Grammar*, *How to Teach Grammar*, *How to Teach Vocabulary*, and a grammar practice book for students, *Natural Grammar*. More recently he has taken an active interest in online learning, having overseen the writing of a five-level internet-delivered course in general English.

Alan Maley worked for The British Council from 1962 to 1988, serving as English Language Officer in Yugoslavia, Ghana, Italy, France, and China, and as Regional Representative in South India (Madras). From 1988 to 1993 he was Director-General of the Bell Educational Trust, Cambridge. From 1993 to 1998 he was Senior Fellow in the Department of English Language and Literature of the National University of Singapore, and from 1998 to 2002 he was Director of the graduate programme at Assumption University, Bangkok. He is currently a freelance consultant. Among his publications are *Literature*, in this series, *Beyond Words*, *Sounds Interesting*, *Sounds Intriguing*, *Words*, *Variations on a Theme*, and *Drama Techniques in Language Learning* (all with Alan Duff), *The Mind's Eye* (with Françoise Grellet and Alan Duff), *Learning to Listen*, and *Poem into Poem* (with Sandra Moulding), *Short and Sweet*, and *The English Teacher's Voice*.

Foreword

Grammar, like death and taxes, is one of the few certainties in the life of a language teacher. It is the subject we love to hate. Many teachers feel uncomfortable with having to live with it, yet instinctively know they cannot live without it. For other teachers, grammar is the only secure point in the seeming chaos of communicative uncertainty, and they cling to it for safety. Whatever our feelings about grammar, it is clear that it is one (but only one) of the pillars which support a language. Without it, we are reduced to a kind of phrase-book pidgin. Yet the problem of just how to approach the teaching of grammar remains.

The book attempts to grasp this particular nettle. Rather than advocating any single approach, the author's objective has been to raise teachers' awareness of the many options open to them for the teaching of this problematic area. He has made a judicious selection of activities and techniques ranging from highly traditional, form-focused activities, through more personalized, communicative tasks, to activities based on the use of language games. It is hoped that, offered this rich menu of varied activities, teachers will be able to choose those which best suit their particular classroom context, and personal teaching preference.

Perhaps the most innovative feature of the book is its overall organization. The author has chosen to discriminate between three kinds of grammar: word grammar, sentence grammar, and text grammar, and to use this division as the organizing principle for the structure of the book.

The work on computer corpora over the past decade or two has taught us a great deal about the systematic behaviour of **words** in context. This finely-tuned system operates at the hazy borderline between lexis and grammar, and merits much more attention than it has so far received. **Sentence** grammar is, of course, the core of most treatments of grammar in foreign language contexts. It is the staple of most textbooks, and many reference works. Clearly, no treatment of grammar could afford to neglect it. **Text** grammar has emerged in recent years from work on discourse analysis, as it has become clear that sentences have not only to be 'correct' but also to 'fit' both the context and co-text in which they occur. A sensitivity to the way sentences function as part of a text is another indispensable aspect of grammatical command. It therefore finds its rightful place in this book.

Teachers will appreciate the author's clarity of explanation, and the lightness of touch with which he has dealt with this most contentious of subjects. The book will, we hope, prove a valued resource in the teaching of grammar for many years to come.

Alan Maley

Introduction

Why a book on grammar?

Grammar generates more 'heat' among language teachers than perhaps any other teaching issue. A quick trawl through some of the postings on a language teaching website on the topic of grammar teaching—for example, the OUP Teacher's Club at http://www.oup.com/elt/global/teachersclub/teaching/debate/grammar—gives some indication as to the range of opinions that exists:

- A lot of people can speak foreign languages fluently, but very few of them can speak foreign languages perfectly. Grammar IS very important, because it helps people to use a language much more correctly.
- I think you can get away with a communicative approach to teach English—remember little children in native [English] speaking countries don't study grammar and learn the language.
- Grammar should, no, must be learnt. I have students from different secondary schools and to start talking isn't so difficult. But what language! Just words joined together.
- Let's teach the importance of using words to form sentences, rather than grammar itself as some kind of mathematical equation.
- I think grammar should be taught just to elicit differences in use from your students' mother tongue. I've tried to let them deduce such differences from examples.
- Sometimes you get the feeling that the students won't dare open their mouths unless they know a grammar rule! Grammar should only be taught on 'a need to know basis' and should be taught in context.
- I have always found teaching grammar through conversation (without them even noticing it) the best way!
- I totally agree that grammar is very important for the basis of a good learning in English and other languages. From that basis we can learn all the rest. But we need to pay attention that nowadays students want even more dynamic classes, where conversation is of top interest.

It is not the purpose of this book to attempt to resolve the many issues that fuel the 'grammar debate'. Nevertheless, devoting a whole book to grammar teaching activities, in a series that offers 'practical guidance in key aspects of language teaching', suggests, at the very least, that a certain importance is attached to grammar, and that therefore it is worthy of attention. What is this importance, and is this attention justified?

To answer these questions, it is necessary to look at what grammar *does*. Grammar is the process by which language is organized and patterned in order to make meaning. At the level of the sentence, this involves the way the elements in a sentence are ordered, such as the fact that (in English) the **subject** precedes the **verb**, and the **object** follows it, as in *the man–bite–the dog*. The rules associated with this grammar function are what traditionally come under the heading of *syntax*. **Syntax** describes the way words are organized into sentences. Then there are the rules by which the words are made to relate to one another in order to fine-tune meaning even further, for example, *The man bites the dog* vs *The man was bitten by the dog*. This fine-tuning is often achieved by different word forms (*bite, bites, bitten*), the rules of which are the concern of **morphology**. The ordering and fine-tuning of these sentence elements constitutes what, in this book, we will call *sentence grammar*. Sentence grammar has always been the traditional domain of both grammar description and teaching, and Part 2 on Sentence Grammar comprises the bulk of the activities.

But there is another level of organization of language, and that is the way that specific words, often with similar meanings, have associated patterns. Thus, *by* is frequently found after **past participles** (*bitten by …, written by …, directed by …*) as a way of indicating the agent of the action: *The man was bitten by the dog*. And *by* is often followed by **nouns** like *car, bus, train,* and *mule*, to say how someone or something is transported. It can also be followed by an *-ing* form, such as *going* or *writing*, and it forms the first element in set phrases such as *by the way, by and large*, and so on. It should be obvious that this level of grammar encroaches on what is traditionally thought of as *vocabulary*. For this reason, we will call it *word grammar*.

But grammar also functions at a level beyond words and sentences. Grammar operates at the level of connected sentences in order to make texts both cohesive and coherent. (A text is cohesive if its elements are connected; it is coherent if it makes sense.) In the example that follows, the choice between sentence 1 and sentence 2 as possible ways of completing the text is determined not by factors internal to the sentence (since both sentences are 'correct') but by the larger context:

> *A man and a woman sustained light injuries yesterday when they were attacked by their household pets.*
>
> 1 *The dog bit the man.*
>
> 2 *The man was bitten by the dog.*
>
> *The woman was scratched by the cat.*

In the interests of topic consistency over the three sentences, and according to the principle of '**end-weight**', whereby new information is placed at the end of the sentence, sentence 2 is the preferred choice here. The way that grammatical choices both determine, and are determined by, the surrounding text we will call *text grammar*.

The interaction of these three levels of grammar—word, sentence, and text—provides a range of resources for making meaning that enhances the subtlety and precision of language in use. While it is true that it is possible to communicate fairly effectively by simply stringing words together, as in *man bite dog*, most learners are keen to graduate from this somewhat pidginized way of speaking, especially when misunderstandings result, as might be the case had they meant to say *The man was bitten by the dog*. This is where grammar, at all its levels, comes into play. Grammar is a way of reducing ambiguity.

Grammar also has a social function: the particular grammar you adopt, like the particular accent you use, distinguishes you as part of a social group (or discourse community). This is why so much ink is expended on issues like *isn't* vs *ain't*, *fewer* vs *less* (as in *There were fewer/less people here than last time)*, and **pronouns**, as in *He is taller than I/me*. Here there is no question of ambiguity, but simply one of group membership: are you in or out? For learners who aspire to be members of an educated, native-speaker-like, discourse community, then third person *-s*, and the standard use of the **present perfect**, will be important. For those who don't, they won't.

Finally, grammar has a testing function: that is to say, it is used as a measure of language proficiency much more commonly than, say, fluency, or vocabulary knowledge. For learners who want to pass exams, grammar will be a priority.

For all these reasons, the centrality of grammar in language teaching and learning is incontestable. More controversial is how, and how often, grammar should be dealt with, in the classroom.

The aims of this book

We have already said that, apart from recognizing the centrality of grammar in language use, this book does not take sides in the grammar debate. Rather, it is aimed at raising teachers' awareness as to the *how* of grammar teaching, and the wide range of classroom options that are available. These options are both more varied and more informed than they once were, when grammar teaching was very much determined (and constrained) by the prevailing 'method' of the day, be it direct method, audiolingualism, or communicative language teaching. Now, in what has been called the 'post-method' era, many teachers feel less compelled to teach 'by the book', as it were, and are freer to adapt their approach to suit their specific needs.

This does not mean, though, that it is simply a case that 'anything goes', and that teaching ideas can be plucked off the shelf at random. Teachers need to evaluate any teaching option or resource in terms of its relevance, appropriacy, and practicability in their particular teaching context. Teachers of young learners, for example, will need to approach the teaching of grammar with care, since activities that might suit an adult class, such as those which require a knowledge of *metalanguage* (that is, grammar terminology), will probably be unsuitable for five-year-olds. By the same token, an activity that involves performing actions (such as Total Physical Response—see Activity 2.16) might not go down well with an advanced class of business students.

Nevertheless, the measure of a useful classroom activity is the extent to which it can be adapted for different purposes and for use in different contexts. The activities in this book have been chosen because they are *generic*—that is, they provide you with a template for an activity type that can be adapted to suit a range of objectives and circumstances. Activities that target just one aspect of grammar, or just one kind of context, have been excluded, and, even if an activity is explained with reference to a specific grammar item, suggestions are provided as to how the activity can be adapted towards other ends.

Thus it is hoped that, by following and adapting the activities, you will augment and enhance your grammar teaching capability exponentially. In this sense, then, the book is less a *resource* book, than a book that will help make teachers more *resourceful.*

Who is this book for?

This book is for both inexperienced and experienced teachers, i.e. those at the very outset of their career, who are coping with the demands of teaching grammar for the first time, as well as for teachers with some classroom experience but who may feel the need to extend their repertoire of grammar teaching techniques. Inevitably, grammar terminology is used throughout, but terms are clearly explained within the text or in the Glossary at the end of the book.

How is the book organized?

Following the three-way distinction made earlier, the book's three Parts deal with *word grammar, sentence grammar,* and *text grammar,* in that order. That is, Part 1 on Word Grammar deals with the grammar of words, and the way words can be combined following grammatical principles. Part 2 on Sentence Grammar looks at the way sentences are constructed, again according to grammatical principles. Finally, Part 3 on Text Grammar explores the interrelation between grammar and stretches of discourse that are larger than the sentence.

Within these broad divisions, activities are mutually independent, and you should not feel compelled to work through them in a set order. Nor has any attempt been made to group activities according to the traditional labels of *presentation, practice,* and *production.* This is partly because the so-called 'PPP' model is too closely associated with a particular methodology, and, as mentioned earlier, this book aspires to transcend a 'method' view of teaching. But also, it is because a 'presentation' activity in one context may work equally well as a 'practice' one in another—and vice versa. In fact, given the exposure to English that most learners have already had, it is seldom very clear or predictable what is *new* to them, hence the whole idea of 'presentation' is somewhat problematic. It is more often the case that features of English grammar lurk somewhere just beyond learners' conscious awareness, and that your job, therefore, is to help them to *notice* these features. This is why you will find the term 'to raise awareness' used in this book more often than 'to present'.

'Practice' is an equally problematic term, and covers a huge and diverse range of activities, some of which are aimed at accuracy, others at fluency; some at recognition, and others at production; some at learning, and others at testing. So, again, the term is used sparingly. In the Aims section of each activity, the term 'to practise' is generally avoided, in favour of a more specific description of the activity's purpose. Finally, it is up to you to decide when and how to use these activities in your lessons, and these decisions should, of course, take account of the local circumstances and needs.

How is each activity organized?

Each activity is organized under the following headings:

Level

This usually indicates the minimum level that an activity is recommended for, but this will depend in part on the choice of grammar item that is being targeted, which in turn will usually be determined by your syllabus or coursebook. Some of the activities use texts that are pitched at a certain level, but a different choice of text would make the activity suitable for another level altogether.

Time

This is a very approximate guide. Activities that are timed to last from five to ten minutes are typically warm-up activities, but the bulk of the activities extend from twenty to thirty minutes, and some would constitute a whole lesson in many teaching contexts.

Aims

These are expressed in general terms, irrespective of the particular grammar point that you might be teaching. This is because the activities have been chosen on the grounds that they are adaptable to a wide range of grammar points. In the Comments section you will often find suggestions as to which grammar points are particularly suited to the activity, apart, that is, from the point that is used as an example.

Materials

If there are any special materials needed—such as card or adhesive—these will be listed here.

Preparation

This is what you will need to plan in advance of the lesson. It may involve finding or writing anything from a single sentence to a complete text. There are always examples for you to work from.

Procedure

This shows, in numbered stages, how to carry out the activity in class.

Variations

These include ideas on how to adapt the activity to suit different levels or different types of class, and on alternative ways of delivering the activity.

Follow-ups

These are optional extra activities that you can use in the same lesson, or as homework tasks, or in subsequent lessons.

Comments

Here you will find further information about the theoretical background to the activity, or suggestions as to how the activity can be adapted to different contexts or grammar items.

How to use this book

Most teachers will be teaching to a pre-set syllabus, and this syllabus will typically be organized around a list of grammar items. An obvious way, therefore, of using this book is to turn to the list of grammar items in the Index on page 132, and simply look for the 'structure of the day'. However, this rather literal approach ignores the point made earlier, that the activities have been chosen because of their *generative* potential. That is to say, even if an activity is explained by reference to a specific grammar item (such as the **present perfect**, or **modal verbs** of probability), the activity should be easily adaptable to suit other linguistic objectives. Likewise, some activities include example texts, but there is no reason (apart from convenience) that you should feel restricted to the particular choice of text. Most coursebook reading passages and many authentic texts will be suitable for the kinds of activities that require a text.

A less systematic but perhaps more rewarding approach might be to skim through the list of activity titles until you light on something that 'feels right' for the class you have in mind—both in terms of the syllabus requirements you are working under, and also the age, level, and general temperament of the learners themselves. Only by trying out activities can you ever be sure that they will be effective, and therefore worth incorporating into your repertoire of classroom routines.

The Glossary on pages 129–31 explains grammatical terminology. First and major mentions of terms listed in the Glossary are in **bold** in the text.

For grammatical terms which are not in the Glossary, see one of the grammar books recommended in Further Reading (page 128).

1 Word grammar

Introduction

Words have grammar. That claim may seem at odds with the traditional division of language systems into *vocabulary*, on the one hand, and *grammar*, on the other. Grammar has for a long time been regarded as operating principally at the level of the sentence, with words as simply those optional elements that could be fitted into pre-established grammatical 'slots'. For example, students might be taught the form of the **present continuous**, using as an example the sentence *Kim's writing a letter.* They are then asked to produce sentences based on this model, by slotting in these words: *Robin, reading, a book, The children, a story, listening to,* etc.

Of course, it has always been recognized that words are tightly constrained in terms of which slot in a sentence they can fit into. **Nouns** can't go into the **verb** slot, and vice versa. (The fact that ambiguous sentences like *I don't like visiting aunts* are so rare would seem to confirm, rather than disprove, this argument.) The notion that words can be classified according to the slot that they can go into—i.e. that there are *parts of speech,* such as **nouns**, **verbs**, **adjectives**, and so on—is part of the grammar of words.

But there is more to it than that. Some of these word classes, such as nouns, verbs, and adjectives are *open classes*: that is, their membership is potentially unlimited, and proof of this are such recent inventions as *blog, yuppify, hip hop,* and *air bag.*

Other word classes, such as **pronouns**, **determiners**, **prepositions**, and **conjunctions**, are *closed classes,* that is, their membership is limited—in some cases, such as pronouns, *very* limited—and new items cannot just be invented. This is basically because they function as **grammar words**. That is, unlike open class words, they have no 'dictionary' meaning, but serve more to provide the grammatical 'glue' that holds the **content words** together. Unsurprisingly, the grammar words are extremely common. In fact, the fifty most common words in English—apart from one (*said*)—are all grammar words. (For a list of these words, see 100 Most Frequent Words page 133). What's more, these grammar words have enormous coverage. They make up a third to a half of all text. That is to say, every second or third word in a text is likely to be a grammar word. (The grammar words in the last sentence are underlined.) The high frequency of grammar words in English is partly due to the fact that English is not a very inflected language. That is to say, only a little of its grammar is conveyed by means of changes to word endings. In short, the grammar of English resides in its little words.

But there is still more to it than that. Even content words have grammar. Take the verb *to tell.* Note that a sentence such as *She tells,* on its own, is most unlikely. This is because part of the grammar of *tell* is that it must have an **object**. The object can be a kind of speech event, like *a joke, a story,* or *lies,* as in *She tells lies.* On the other hand, the object of *tell* can be a person, but not persons on their own. *She tells me* is as unlikely as *She tells.* Another object is needed, as in *She tells me everything.* Or it can be a *that*-**clause**: *She tells me that you are seeing someone.* These syntactic structures are part of the grammar of *tell*: once you embark on a sentence beginning *She tells …* your choices are highly constrained. They are also constrained if you begin the sentence with *she says,* but they are constrained differently. For a start, you can't say *She says me* or *She says me that you are seeing someone.* The grammar of *say* is different from the grammar of *tell.*

Knowing the grammar of words is as important as knowing the grammar of sentences. In fact, many of the mistakes that learners make, such as *I am writing for ask you …* or *I suggest to you to visit me …* are directly attributable to faulty word grammar.

The activities in Part 1, then, are aimed at raising awareness of, and practising, aspects of word grammar.

1.1 Language bingo

Level Any

Time 20–30 minutes

Aims To teach and check knowledge of basic grammar terminology.

Preparation

Choose about twelve to fifteen familiar words that will serve as examples of different grammar terms. If possible, the words should not belong to more than one class.

Example

Liverpool	(proper noun)
child	(countable noun)
water	(uncountable noun)
sunny	(adjective)
is	(auxiliary verb)
can	(modal verb)
(to) take	(infinitive)
raining	(present participle)
says	(present tense verb)
went	(past tense verb)
forgotten	(past participle)
the	(definite article)
a	(indefinite article)
slowly	(adverb)

and	(conjunction)
from	(preposition)
she	(pronoun)

Procedure

1 Teach some basic grammar terminology. For example, write a sentence on the board, such as: *The sun was shining brightly and I watched a large bird dive into the water.*

2 Ask learners to identify the part of speech of each word in the sentence. Teach the terminology that they don't know. Write the terms below the words in the sentence, like this:

The	*sun*	*was*	*shining*	*brightly*	*and*	*I*	*watched*
(definite) article	(countable) noun	(auxiliary) verb	verb (present participle)	adverb	conjunction	pronoun	verb (past tense)

a	*large*	*bird*	*dive*	*into*	*the*	*water*
(indefinite) article	adjective	(countable) noun	verb (infinitive)	preposition article	(definite) noun	(uncountable)

3 Write the list of words and grammar terms that you have prepared (see above) on the board.

4 Ask the learners to draw a grid with nine squares:

5 Ask them each to choose nine words from the list on the board and to write them into the grid.

6 Read out the different grammar terms, in no particular order, and, as each term is read out, the learners cross out the appropriate word in their grid. For example, if they hear 'definite article', they cross out *the*. Keep a note of the terms that you call out.

7 The first learner to have crossed out all their words, shouts *Bingo!* (or, if you like, *Lingo!*).

8 Go back over the terms that you called out, and, using the list on the board, check that the different grammar terms have been properly matched.

Comments

The terminology that you choose to focus on should consist of only those terms that you feel will be useful for your learners to know. Many learners will already be familiar with these concepts in their own language. For those who are not, and especially for younger learners, you will need to be careful not to overload them.

1.2 Grammar poems

Level Intermediate and above

Time 20–25 minutes

Aims To reinforce grammar terms through creative writing.

Preparation

Prepare a poem 'rubric' (i.e. the framework for a poem) that consists solely of parts of speech.

Example

1 article + noun
2 participle, participle, participle
3 adjective, adjective
4 repeat 1
5 pronoun + verb
6 pronoun + verb
7 pronoun + always/never/still + verb
8 repeat 1
9 repeat 3
10 repeat 2

Procedure

1. Write the rubric on the board, and check that the learners are familiar with the names of the different parts of speech.
2. Tell them that this is the model for a poem. The first line is the title of the poem, for example: *The Sea, A Forest, The Sharks*, etc.
3. Learners work individually or in pairs to compose their poems.
4. They then exchange poems, or the poems can be illustrated and displayed around the room. Here, for example, is a poem that is based on the above rubric:

Example **The Sea**

Smiling, frowning, laughing
Angry, joyful
The sea
It comes
It goes
It never sleeps
The sea
Angry, joyful
Smiling, frowning, laughing

Follow-up

Rub the rubric off the board, and see if the learners can reconstruct it, using their own poems as a guide.

1.3 Count and classify

Level Any

Time 20–50 minutes

Aims To exploit a short text in order to draw attention to the different word classes.

Preparation

Choose a short text, either authentic—such as a postcard from a friend, a short poem, a joke—or a text from the coursebook that the class is using. (See, for example, the sample text below, a poem (of just thirty-nine words) that would be suitable for intermediate learners.)

Procedure

1 Distribute the text. If this is the first time that learners have met the text, give them time to read it and then check their overall understanding by asking, for instance: *What kind of text is it? Who wrote it? Who to? Why? What's it about?* Check any unfamiliar vocabulary.

2 Ask learners to turn the text over. Ask them to paraphrase or translate the text from memory. This will give you an idea of the level of understanding. It may be necessary to return to the text to check details so as to ensure understanding is optimal.

3 Now that the text is intelligible, learners count different word types and classify them according to grammatical categories. The amount of detail you go into will depend on the level of the learners, their familiarity with grammar terminology, the length and difficulty of the text, and your own syllabus requirements. At a very general level, the task you set them might be:

Count the words in the text and classify them.

(Point out that the learners themselves can choose how to classify them.)

More specifically, it might be:

Count the nouns in the text and classify them.
Count the verbs in the text and classify them.
Count the adjectives in the text and classify them.
etc.

At a still greater level of detail, and for more advanced learners, you could dictate—or write on the board or on to a worksheet—a selection of the following questions:

1. How many words are there in the text?
2. Which of these words are repeated?
3. How many different parts of speech are represented (i.e. nouns, verbs, adjectives, adverbs, pronouns, determiners, prepositions, and conjunctions)?
4. Of the nouns, which are countable and which are uncountable?
5. Count the verbs. Which are transitive (they take an object) and which are intransitive (they don't take an object)?
6. Classify the verb phrases—for example, according to tense (present or past) or aspect (continuous or perfect)?
7. Identify any pronouns—what are their referents (i.e. the people or things they refer to)?
8. Identify any conjunctions, and classify them; for example, are they additive (like *and*) or contrastive (like *but*)?
9. What is the proportion of grammar words (such as articles, conjunctions, pronouns, prepositions, and auxiliary verbs) and content words (such as nouns, adjectives, verbs, and adverbs)?

Learners can work individually, and then check in pairs or small groups, or work in pairs/small groups from the outset. It may help to allow learners to consult grammar reference books and/or dictionaries, while doing the task.

Sample text **Walking at Dusk**

Wonderful long evenings!
I walk slowly about, carrying an old stick.
The moon calms its part of the sky.
White clouds roll and do not move.
The cows seem to be growing out of the field.

(Robert Bly. *Silence in the Snowy Fields and Other Poems.* London: Jonathan Cape, 1967)

Comments

The activity demonstrates that a text, even a very short one, yields an enormous amount of grammar information. Even at the level of classifying the word classes in the Robert Bly poem (above) the following facts come to light:

Word	Word class
Walking	**verb** (**intransitive**, non-finite, **present participle**)
at	**preposition** (time)
dusk	**noun** (**uncountable**, singular)
Wonderful	**adjective** (ungradable*)
long	adjective (gradable*)
evenings	noun (**countable**, plural)
I	**pronoun** (personal, subject)
walk	verb (intransitive, finite, present tense)
slowly	**adverb** (of manner)
about	adverb (of place)
carrying	verb, non-finite, present participle
an	**article** (indefinite)
old	adjective (gradable)
stick	noun (countable, singular)
The	article (definite)
moon	noun (countable, singular)
calms	verb (transitive, **finite**, present tense)
its	**possessive determiner**
part	noun (countable, singular)
of	**preposition** (of attribute)
the	article (definite)
sky	noun (uncountable, singular)
White	adjective (gradable)
clouds	noun (countable, plural)
roll	verb (intransitive, finite, present tense)
and	**conjunction** (additive)
do	**auxiliary verb**, present
not	adverb (negative **particle**)
move	verb (intransitive, non-finite, **infinitive**)
The	article (definite)
cows	noun (countable, plural)
seem	verb (intransitive, finite, present tense)
to	infinitive particle
be	verb (intransitive, non-finite, **infinitive**)
growing	verb (intransitive, non-finite, present participle)
out	preposition (of place)
of	preposition (part of preposition phrase *out of*)
the	article (definite)
field	noun (countable, singular)

* A gradable adjective can be used with a word like *very* to say that the person or thing referred to has more or less of a quality, for example *very hungry, rather cold*. An adjective like *perfect* or *dead* is ungradable so cannot normally be used with words like *very*, because the quality either exists or it doesn't.

Note that in other contexts, some of these words would function differently. Thus *sky*, for example, is **countable** in some contexts (*They are forecasting sunshine and clear blue skies*) and the verb *to grow* can also be **transitive**.

Follow-up

1 Having subjected the text to such close analysis, the learners may be ready to re-construct it from memory. One way of doing this is to give them the words of the text, in alphabetical order, and set them the task of re-assembling the text. A competitive element could be introduced by dividing the class into teams and turning the activity into a race. Here is the text (including its title) 'de-constructed':

> about an and at be calms carrying clouds cows do dusk evenings field growing I its long moon move not of of old out part roll seem sky slowly stick the the the the to walk walking white wonderful

2 Choose another text of approximately the same length, and subject it to the same kind of analysis. Ask the learners to note any similarities and differences between the number and type of word classes, and the ratio of **grammar words** to **content words**. Ask them to suggest reasons for the similarities and differences. (Most written texts comprise at least one-third grammar words and two-thirds content words. In spoken texts the ratio can be 50:50.)

1.4 Content or grammar words?

Level Pre-intermediate and above

Time 20–30 minutes

Aims To draw attention to the difference between content words (that carry the main information load in a sentence or text) and grammar words (whose function is largely grammatical).

Preparation

Choose a short text which the learners haven't seen before.

Example

> A man went into a pub with his dog and ordered a drink. Then he and the dog started playing darts! 'Hey, that's amazing!' said the barman. 'Your dog can play darts!' 'It's not that amazing,' replied the man. 'In the last ten games he's only beaten me twice!'
>
> (B. Girling. *The Great Puffin Joke Directory*. Penguin Books, 1990)

Prepare two versions of the text, ideally on an overhead projector transparency, one version showing only the **grammar words**, and the other only the **content words**. (You should de-contract any contractions, such as *he's* (= *he has*.)

Grammar words

Example 1 A _____ _____ into a _____ with his _____ and _____ a _____. Then he and the _____ _____ _____ _____! '_____, that is _____!' _____ the _____. 'Your _____ can _____ _____!' 'It is not that _____,' _____ the _____. 'In the _____ _____ _____ he has _____ _____ me _____!'

Content words

2 _____ man went _____ _____ pub _____ _____ dog _____ ordered _____ drink. _____ _____ _____ _____ dog started playing darts! 'Hey, _____ _____ amazing!' said _____ barman. '_____ dog _____ play darts!' '_____ _____ _____ _____ amazing,' replied _____ man. '_____ _____ last ten games _____ _____ only beaten _____ twice!'

Procedure

1 Distribute—or project—the 'grammar words version' of the text. Don't tell learners which version of the text they have. Challenge them to tell you what the text is about. (They won't be able to!)

2 Distribute—or project—the 'content words version'. This time they should not only be able to tell you what kind of text it is and what it is about, but they should also be able to make a good guess at the missing words. Give them time to do this in pairs or small groups.

3 Check the task by allowing them to see the 'grammar words version' again.

4 Ask the learners what different sorts of words comprise each text. (Answer: *grammar words, in text 1*; and *content words in text 2*.)

5 Ask them to tell you what sorts of words are typically grammar words. (Answer: **auxiliary verbs**, **articles**, **pronouns**, **prepositions**, **conjunctions**, **possessive determiners**, and **adverbs** that are not formed from an adjective plus -ly). Ask them what words are typically content words. (Answer: nouns, **lexical** i.e. not auxiliary verbs, adjectives, and adverbs formed from adjective with *-ly*.)

6 Ask learners to estimate the proportion of grammar words to content words in this text. In this text it is 26:26. (There are fifty-two words altogether.) This means that exactly fifty per cent of the text consists of function words.

7 Distribute another text of similar length, and ask learners to identify the grammar words and the content words, and to calculate the proportion of the former to the latter.

Example Here is another text of the same type (with the function words underlined):

> A girl was taking her little brother for a walk in the park. 'Can I go and run along the top of that wall?' he asked her. 'No,' said the sister. 'Go on,' insisted the little boy. 'Well, OK,' she said, 'but if you fall off and break both your legs, don't come running to me.'
>
> (B. Girling. *The Great Puffin Joke Directory*. Penguin Books. 1990)

8 Point out that most texts in English consist roughly half of content words and half of grammar words. To understand texts, we pay attention mainly to the (larger) content words, but to produce texts, we also have to pay attention to the small words, i.e. the grammar words.

Variation 1

1 After Stage 3 above, conceal the grammar word version of the text from the class, and ask them to complete the content word version from memory. Then continue with stage 4.

2 Then conceal the content words version and ask students to complete the grammar word version from memory.

Variation 2

Instead of following stages 1–4, divide the class into pairs and give one member of the pair the grammar word version of the text, and the other member the content word version. They take turns trying to guess what the word is for each blank space in their own version of the text. To make it easier, you could give learners the first sentence in its complete form on the board. To help their guessing strategies, write the following questions on the board:

- Is it a noun/verb/adjective? (etc.)
- Is it an article/pronoun/preposition? (etc.)

Follow-up

Ask learners to collect short texts in English from newspapers, magazines, packaging, the Internet, etc. These can be advertisements, news items, TV film plot summaries, weather reports, etc.—but they should be written in connected sentences, not abbreviated, as in apartment rental ads, for example. They should then prepare a version of the text with all the grammar words gapped out, alongside a list of all the grammar words that have been removed. They then exchange their texts and attempt to complete them.

Example Here, for example, is an art gallery announcement in a magazine for visitors to Cambridge, along with the grammar words that have been extracted from it:

> Fifteen paintings _____ _____ Sudanese School style _____ Abdallah Meirgani _____ exhibited _____ Café Afrika _____ December. Influences _____ architecture, alphabet _____ graffiti, symbols _____ Islam _____ _____ colours _____ Africa _____ depicted _____ art works _____ celebrate _____ vitality _____ Afro-Arab culture.
>
> *and and are are at by in in of of of of the the the throughout which*

Complete text

Fifteen paintings in the Sudanese School style by Abdallah Meirgani are exhibited at Café Afrika throughout December. Influences of architecture, alphabet and graffiti, symbols of Islam and the colours of Africa are depicted in art works which celebrate the vitality of Afro-Arab culture.

(*Explorer*, Issue 16, December 2003)

Comment

The distinction between content words and grammar words is not always a black-and-white one. As a rule of thumb, grammar words are short, high frequency words, especially those belonging to the word classes mentioned above (i.e. auxiliary verbs, articles, pronouns, prepositions, conjunctions, possessive determiners, and adverbs that are not formed from an adjective plus *-ly*). And they often have no direct, one-to-one translation from one language into another. Labelling them precisely is less important than that learners appreciate the important role these 'little words' play in making English grammatical.

1.5 Grammar word brainstorm

Level Intermediate to advanced

Time 20–30 minutes

Aims To sensitize learners to the fact that high-frequency grammar words can have a range of functions.

Preparation

Prepare some sentences for dictation, containing different uses of some high-frequency, multi-use, **grammar words**, such as *is*, *had*, *to*, *it*, *that*, *still*, *since*, *well*, and *so*. A good dictionary will help you with this.

Procedure

1 Learners work in pairs or small groups to brainstorm as many different ways these words can be used. They can either think of examples (without grammatical labels) or grammatical labels and examples, for instance:

is as main verb: *She is 17.*
as auxiliary in present continuous constructions: *It is raining.*
as auxiliary in present **passive** constructions: *English is spoken here.*
as a future form, with *to-* infinitive: *The PM is to fly to Brussels.*

2 Dictate some sentences that include these words, which learners write down and then either match with the categories they have already come up with, or use to create new categories, for example:

had *When we arrived the film had already started.* (**auxiliary verb, past perfect**)
My grandparents had ten children. (**main verb**, **past simple**)
I had to work on Saturday. (**modal auxiliary**; past)
They've had the house painted. (causative *have*, past participle)
If I had more time, I'd learn a language. (main verb; unreal *if* clause)

to *We got lost on the way to the beach.* (preposition of place)
It's ten to six. (preposition of time)
To be or not to be. (infinitive marker)

it *I had a dog but it ran away.* (**subject pronoun**)
I had an umbrella but I lost it. (**object pronoun**)
It started to rain. (impersonal subject pronoun)

that *Did you see that car?* (**determiner**)
What's that on your arm? (pronoun)
I enjoyed the CD that you gave me. (**relative pronoun**)
I remembered that it was her birthday. (conjunction)

still *Is it still raining?* (adverb)
The holiday was expensive. Still, it was worth it. (**linker**)

well *I'm not very well.* (adjective)
How well can you dance? (adverb)
Well, isn't this nice? (**discourse marker**)

so *It was late so we took a taxi.* (linker)
She is so tall that people stare at her. (adverb of degree)
My sister is married and so is my brother. (adverb substituting for a clause)
So, this is your apartment. (discourse marker)

3 Learners then write a dialogue, incorporating as many possible uses of these words as they can in the one dialogue, which they can then read aloud—or act out—to the rest of the class.

1.6 Dictionary grammar

Level Intermediate and above

Time 20–30 minutes

Aims To use dictionary examples as a source for word grammar awareness-raising.

Materials A learner's dictionary that has sentence-length citations (that is, examples of words in context), such as the *Oxford Advanced Learner's Dictionary* (*OALD*); enough copies to distribute to the class, at least one per group of three students. Optional: a transparency showing a dictionary entry for a grammar word.

Preparation

Four or five citations from the dictionary entry for a **grammar word**, with the keyword gapped out.

Procedure

1 Demonstrate the activity by writing on the board prepared sentences that have been taken out of a dictionary entry for a common grammar word, leaving a blank at each place where the word occurs.

Example The following sentences come from the *Oxford Advanced Learner's Dictionary* (7th edition) under the entry for *own*.

It was her _____ idea.
Our children are grown up and have children of their _____.
I need a room of my _____.
She makes all her _____ clothes.
Do you _____ your house or do you rent it?

2 Ask learners to guess what the missing word is. Don't forget to tell them that it is the same in each sentence. If they cannot guess straight away, ask them to think of what part of speech it might be—it may be different in different sentences—and whether they can discern any similarities in meaning across the sentences. Once they have guessed, show where the sentences came from, if possible, by projecting a photocopy of the dictionary entry using an overhead projector.

3 Distribute dictionaries to learners who work in pairs or small groups. Either assign words (see the list of 100 Most Frequent Words on page 127, for example), or ask learners to choose their own (but check that the words that they have chosen are either grammar words, or very high frequency words like *get*, *way*, *thing*, etc.). The words should be different for each group and should be kept secret. Learners prepare gap-fill sentences, using the citations in the dictionary under the word. Point out that they should prepare four to six sentences, and these should include a representative spread of the meanings from the entry. Encourage them to first skim through the dictionary entry (which might be quite long) in order to get a feel for the different meanings. Groups that finish early can be given another word to do.

4 Groups then exchange their sentences, and have to work out what the missing word is. They can consult the dictionaries to check.

Variation 1

Rather than copy the dictionary citations verbatim, ask learners to use them to make their own gap-fill sentences which embody a range of different senses and uses of the target word. This will ensure they devote some attention to the meaning of the citations.

Variation 2

If learners don't have access to a dictionary with sentence-length citations but instead have access to dictionaries with only definitions, ask them to use the information in the definitions to make their own sentences. These should be checked for accuracy, though, before being turned into a gap-fill.

Follow-up 1

Learners could also attempt to classify the different uses of the target word, and then check with the dictionaries. Basic categories will include part of speech, and meaning.

Follow-up 2

Learners could then write true sentences—about themselves or their classmates, for example—based on each of the different uses of the target word.

1.7 Do-it-yourself concordancing

Level Elementary and above

Time 30–45 minutes

Aims To sensitize learners to the grammar words in English, their frequency, and their multiple uses.

Preparation

Choose a text, either authentic or from a coursebook, of at least 200 words in length. Use a text that learners are already familiar with. It could be an authentic text. Or it could be a reading passage, or a transcript of a listening passage, from the coursebook. It is important that the text is as natural as possible, i.e. that it hasn't been specially written to display a particular grammar feature. (The sample text below, a 219-word transcript from *natural English Intermediate* would be suitable.) Make copies of the text and distribute these to the class.

Procedure

1 To demonstrate the activity, and to show what *concordancing* involves, choose a **grammar word** that occurs with relatively high frequency in the text, write it on the board, and ask the learners to tell you how many times it occurs.

2 Then ask them to tell you the words that occur on either side of it, up to about six. This context should be sufficient to demonstrate the grammar pattern the word is embedded in at the **phrase** or **clause** level, and to give enough context for the meaning to be easily retrievable.

3 Write these contexts on to the board, arranging them in lines and so that the keyword is aligned down the centre. This example is taken from the sample text below:

```
        last year, when I was IN India,
we asked this man to take us IN his coracle
              so we stepped IN very carefully,
       there were three of us IN this boat
         water started coming IN (Oh no!)
```

(These are called *concordance lines*.)

4 Ask learners if they can identify any patterns in the lines that are displayed. For example, three of the examples of *in* above are followed by a place, in the form of a **noun phrase** (*India, his coracle, this boat*), while the other two are not. These two are in turn preceded by a **verb** (*stepped, coming*). You could point out that, where *in* is followed by a noun, it is functioning as a preposition. But where *in* is not followed by a noun, and it is preceded by a verb, it is functioning as an **adverb**—as the **adverbial particle** of a **phrasal verb**, in fact.

5 Now, ask learners to work individually or in pairs to prepare their own concordance lines based on the text. Depending on what you choose to be your focus, either assign different words to different pairs, or assign the same words to all pairs. Choose words that occur at least three times in the text, and (for the purposes of this task) make sure they are grammar words. In the example text above, the following words might usefully be studied: *go* (and *going*), *really*, *so*, and *was*. Here, for instance, are concordance lines for *so* (from the sample text below):

```
                     and SO we asked this man to take us
                and erm, SO we stepped in very carefully
                  it was SO peaceful and quiet
                     and SO our little boat started
                            going round
we managed to get out, SO it was, it was exciting
```

6 When the learners have prepared their concordance lines, they should then start looking for patterns. To do this, it will help if they look at the words immediately to the left and to the right of the keyword, and try to identify what part of speech it is. They should also be warned that there may only be one pattern in the (relatively limited number of) lines that they have.

7 If learners have been working on different words, they could write their concordance lines on to an overhead projector transparency, and then can take turns to 'explain' their lines to the rest of the class. If they have been working on the same words, they could exchange lines and classifications, and compare their answers.

Sample text Well, erm, last year, when I was in India, erm, myself and my boyfriend wanted to go from one side of the river to the other side of the river (Mm) and so we asked this man to take us in his coracle—which is, I don't know if you know what they are (No!) but they're a tiny boat, they're circular, almost like erm, a dish really (Oh) and erm, so we stepped in very carefully, there were three of us in this boat and erm, off we went, and it was just beautiful, it was so peaceful and quiet and all we could hear was the water, and it was a really beautiful experience (Yeah) until suddenly the water started whirling round and round and round, and so our little boat started going round and round, and we were really frightened because water started coming in (Oh no!) to the coracle and it was going faster and faster, and the man seemed out of control and we could hear the water and it was splashing us (Ah!) and we seemed to be sinking (Oh) and eventually he pulled us to the side and er, we managed to get out, so it was, it was exciting and it was different, but erm, it was a bit too frightening.

(*Natural English Intermediate Listening Booklet*. Oxford University Press, 2002)

Variation

The concordance lines can be used to make sentence gap-fills, with the keyword blanked out, which can then be exchanged with other groups, who have to guess what the missing word is, as in Activity 1.6 *Dictionary grammar*, above.

Comments

1 The classification of concordance lines can, of course, be done by consulting dictionaries and grammars.

2 This activity has focused solely on grammar words, but other high frequency words, such as high frequency verbs, like *take*, *make*, and *get*, and high frequency nouns, like *way*, *thing*, and *place*, could also be targeted.

Follow-up

This activity is a good way of introducing learners to the idea of keeping a *Keyword Notebook*—that is, a notebook in which they record examples of the high frequency words in English, one word per page. As they encounter new instances of these words (in their classroom work or outside the classroom), they can add lines to their concordances, and even number them according to the use each example represents. For example in^1 = preposition; in^2 = adverb.

Comments

A list of the top 100 most frequent words in English can be found on page 127.

Acknowledgements

I am grateful to Jane Willis for introducing me to the idea of learners making their own concordances.

1.8 Keyword stories

Level Intermediate to advanced

Time 30–50 minutes

Aims To sensitize learners to the productive power of keywords, and to provide practice in associating these words with their typical grammatical environments.

Materials Dictionaries.

Preparation

1 Choose a keyword—that is a word that has high frequency in English, either because it is a **grammar word** or because it is a highly versatile **content word** (like *take, got, thing, way*). Write a short text that uses this keyword a number of times and in a number of different ways. You can consult the entries in a dictionary for ideas.

Example This sample text below uses *got*.)

> Tom and Liz got on well and in time they got married. But Tom got bored. He got up to no good. One night he got home late. 'You've got lipstick on your collar,' she said. She got to thinking. She got a gun. He got what was coming. She got the first bus out of town. They never got her.

2 Prepare some sentences for dictation that do *not* include the keyword, but which can be paraphrased using the keyword.

Example
She never arrived at work on time. (= She never got to work on time.)
What do you have in your hand? (= What have you got in your hand?)
They enjoyed each other's company. (= They got on well [with each other].)
The children soon became bored. (= The children soon got bored.)
etc.

3 Finally, prepare some sentences that can be paraphrased using another keyword, for example, *take*:

Example
The bus journey was very long. (= The bus journey took a long time)
Please remove your hat. (= Please take off your hat)
Can you photograph me? (= Can you take my photograph?)
I usually go to work by bus. (= I usually take the bus to work)
etc.

Procedure

1 Students read the story, and identify the keyword, that is the word that is significantly prominent, i.e. *got*. (In this case it occurs in every sentence.)

2 Using dictionaries and working in pairs or small groups, they 'unpack' the text, that is, they work out what it means so that they are prepared to give a paraphrase of the story, without using the verb *got*. You can give an example: *Tom and Liz got on well. = Tom and Liz liked each other*. In some cases, the unpacking may only involve substituting the keyword with a synonym, for example *She got the first bus. = She took the first bus*. In others it will mean redrafting the sentence completely, for example *He got up to no good. = He behaved badly*.

3 Individual students take turns to report to the class how their group unpacked each sentence.

4 Students then classify the different uses of *got*. Depending on the level, they can attempt to define the categories themselves, or they can be given the categories in advance:

got + noun phrase
got + participle
got as phrasal verb
have + *got*
got as part of an idiomatic phrase

5 Using dictionaries, they can then add two or three more combinations to each list.

6 Dictate the second set of prepared sentences, and ask the learners to paraphrase them using the keyword (*got*).

7 Dictate the third set of prepared sentences, and ask learners to paraphrase them using another keyword (*take*).

8 Students can then write their own keyword story, using a high frequency verb, such as the one that you chose in stage 7. They will need dictionaries to do this. They can then read and compare each other's stories.

Variation

For Stage 8 above, different groups can be given different keywords. They write their story but leave a gap in place of the keyword. Groups read the stories of other groups, and they have to work out what the missing keyword is.

Follow-up

Show learners how to record the different uses of a keyword in the form of a 'spidergram', for example:

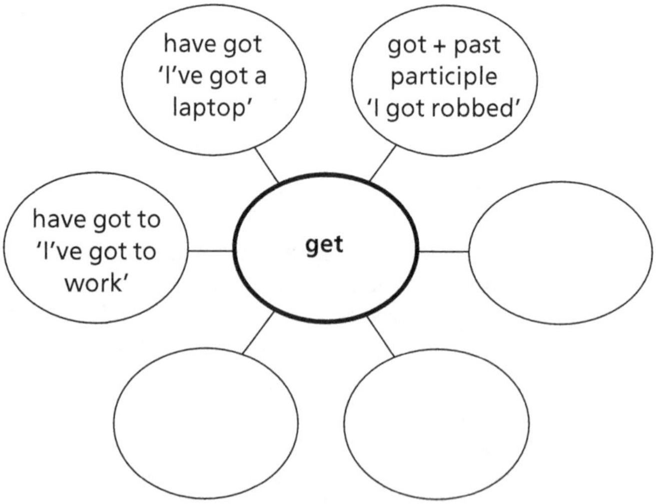

Spidergrams have the advantage over lists in that they can display relationships between uses more clearly and memorably, and new words or uses can be inserted without major disruption to the existing pattern. For these reasons, they provide an effective resource for complementing the information in the *Keyword Notebook*, an idea outlined above, in the Follow-up to Activity 1.7, 'Do-it-yourself concordancing'.

Comments

These keyword stories are designed to display a particular feature of the language in a way that makes it stand out, but they are not of course representative of real texts, where such a high degree of repetition would be unusual.You may wish to make this point to the learners, if it is not already obvious.

1.9 Keyword insertion

Level Intermediate and above

Time 15–25 minutes

Aims To raise awareness about the frequency and multi-functionality of keywords (words that have high frequency in English, either because they are grammar words or because they are highly versatile content words).

Preparation

Prepare a text with all instances of one keyword removed. In the sample text below, all twelve examples of *way* (and *ways*) have been taken out. Make copies for your students.

Procedure

1 Hand out copies of the text, and tell learners that twelve instances of the word *way/ways* have been removed. Working individually, or in pairs or small groups, their task is to re-insert them. So, the first sentence of the sample text below would read: *A neighbour of mine who lives across the way* ... Depending on the level of the class, you may want to let them consult dictionaries as they do the task.

2 Once the task has been completed, check by having learners take turns to read the sentences of the text aloud.

Sample text **My neighbour**

A neighbour of mine who lives across the phoned me to say that he was in a bad. 'Can you stop by on your to work?' he asked. I wouldn't usually go out of my for him, and my first thought was, no. He has been a bad neighbour in more than one. For a start, he always parks his car in the. He's one of those people who like to get their own. He also owes me money, by the. On the other hand, I quite like him, in a strange. And he doesn't have much in the of family or friends, So I thought this might be a good to improve relations ....

Variation

A competitive element can be introduced by turning the task into a race, with the pair or group who are first to complete the task calling out *Bingo!*, for example. Of course, if it is subsequently discovered that that team did not get all the answers correct, the team that got the most right answers is declared the winner instead.

Follow-up 1

Ask learners to classify all the different uses of the keyword, once the words themselves have been reinserted into the text. Or ask them to record them in the form of a spidergram (see Activity 1.8 Follow-up for an example).

Follow-up 2

Ask learners to write their own texts, based around a high frequency word, and then to prepare a version of the text with all instances of that word removed. Learners then exchange texts and 'test' each other. It will help if learners have access to a dictionary when doing this task.

Comments

Such texts are not that difficult to compose, since keywords are—by definition—highly frequent, and therefore even naturally occurring texts are likely to have a high proportion of them. Of course, as in Activity 1.8, 'Keyword stories', a text with a dozen or more of the keywords in it is very contrived, but this does not necessarily detract from its value as a learning tool.

1.10 Odd couples

Level Upper-intermediate to advanced

Time 15–30 minutes

Aims To explore the versatility of high frequency words.

Preparation

Prepare identical sets of word cards, one for each group of three to five students. These should consist of at least 30 cards, each about half the size of a business card, and on each of which is written a high frequency **grammar word** or a high frequency **content word**, so that there are equal proportions of each. The function words and the content words should be distinguished, by a different colour or font:

of	is	did	been	has	in	to	the	by	that
how	my	for	a	what	dog	hit	water	like	often
tree	*child*	*good*	*car*	*long*	*school*	*go*	*took*	*going*	*lost*

Procedure

1 Write *the tree* on the board. Ask the class to give you a sentence with these two words in it, such as *I climbed the tree*. Then write *tree the* on the board, and, again, challenge the class to produce a sentence. If they can't, suggest *This is the tree the cat climbed up*. Explain that the game they are about to play is to try and fit two-word sequences into sentences of their own invention.

2 Put the class into groups of three to five students, and distribute the word card packs, one to each group. Learners should first separate the function words from the content words, making a pack of each. They shuffle the packs and place them face down in front of them.

3 They each take turns to pick up two cards, one from the top of each pack. They have to try to make two sentences incorporating the words in sequence, one sentence with the words in one order (for example, *the tree*), and the other with the words in the reverse order (i.e. *tree the*). They earn a point for each sentence that is judged acceptable by the rest of the group. (The teacher should be prepared to arbitrate in the event of a contested sentence.) Learners may find that sometimes it will not be possible to construct one sentence, let alone two—but the effort in trying to do so should push them to explore the full range of uses of the words in question. Note that the words must be in sequence and cannot be interrupted by another word nor by any form of punctuation. For example, for the words *good* and *is*, *This is good, is it not?* is not acceptable, but *What is good is the service* is acceptable.

4 After each turn the cards are placed at the bottom of their respective packs. And the game continues until all the words have been used. (The game can continue but the cards should then be reshuffled.) The winner is the person who gains the most points after a certain time limit, or after everyone has had a predetermined number of turns.

5 Appoint one student to record all the sentences that are considered acceptable. After the game has finished, some of these sentences can be read out to the class, or written on the board—especially those sentences which show evidence of particular ingenuity.

Variation

With a smaller set of the same cards—say twenty—this game can be played as a form of *Memory* (also called *Pelmanism*). The cards are placed face down, and players take turns to pick up two cards each. If they can successfully make at least one sentence incorporating the two words in sequence, they keep the pair of cards and these cannot be reused. If not, they are turned face down again, in the same place where they came from, and the next player has a turn. Players try to remember which card is which, so that they can reuse them later when they have worked out where viable combinations are. At some point the number of viable combinations will be exhausted, even though there are cards still unused. At this point the players should agree to finish, and to count up the number of pairs they have each won. The player with the most pairs is the winner.

1.11 Sentence creation

Level Intermediate and above

Time 20–30 minutes

Aims To explore the sentence-making potential of a combination of grammar words and content words.

Preparation

Create a set of word cards as in Activity 1.10, i.e. at least thirty cards, each about half the size of a business card, and on each of which is written a high frequency **grammar word** or a high frequency **content word**.

1. Put a full set of cards in a bag or box. Organize the class into teams of three or four.
2. Draw one card out of the bag at a time, at regular ten second intervals, and read it aloud.
3. In their teams, learners write the words down and attempt to use the words that are accumulating to make a sentence. When they think they have formed a sentence, one of their group shouts it out. Alternatively, instead of shouting the sentence out, one member of each team races to the board and writes it on the board.
4. If the proposed sentence is acceptable, i.e. grammatically well formed and makes plausible sense, it earns points for that team. Points are allocated, one per word, multiplied by the number of words. Thus, a three-word sentence earns nine points, a five-word sentence earns twenty-five points. If the sentence is *not* acceptable, points are deducted on the same basis: thus an incorrect four-word sentence earns a penalty of sixteen points.
5. The other teams then cross out, from their lists, the words that have been used.
6. Continue reading out words until the next team comes up with a sentence. Teams can also add words to the ends of existing sentences. So, if the sentence *They are going* is already on the board, and the word *well* comes up, a team can volunteer *They are going well*. They earn the score for the full sentence (i.e. four times four, or sixteen points).
7. When all the words have been read out, and all sentence-making possibilities have been exhausted, the team with the most points is the winner. Teams can use any leftover words to add to sentences that are already on the board.

Follow-up

Teams can write short two- or three-sentence contexts for the sentences they created.

Comments

You can change the cards regularly to include new vocabulary that has come up in class, but there should always be a 50:50 distribution of grammar words and content words.

1.12 Slow-release grammar chunks

Level Beginner to intermediate

Time 20–30 minutes

Aims To encourage the memorization of 'chunks' that contain key grammar structures, which may then become available for later analysis (either conscious or unconscious).

Materials Paper or cardboard for displaying around the classroom walls; marker pens.

Preparation

Prepare some useful classroom language in the form of **chunks**, that is, commonly used phrases or sentences that are still short enough to be easily memorized and reproduced.

Example

I don't know.
I don't understand.
I haven't finished.
I've finished.
Not yet.
It's my turn.
You go first.
How do you spell it?
What does [...] mean?
Could you write it?
I'm sorry.
You're welcome.

Procedure

1 Dictate the sentences.

2 Learners check first the spelling, then the meaning of the chunks they have written down. If they are a monolingual group, elicit translations of each chunk. (It's important that learners are very clear as to the meaning, and the kind of situations in which the chunk is used.)

3 Drill the expressions so that learners can produce them fluently. Pay attention to the correct stress and intonation in the chunk, and make sure that the learners use contractions and weak forms, for example /haʊdəjuːˈspelət/. The chunk should sound as natural and as fluent as possible.

4 Organize the learners into small groups. Distribute the paper (or cardboard) and marker pens. Assign two or three of the chunks to each group, and ask them to write them in big letters so that they can be displayed around the classroom. It's effective if the cards are cut into speech bubbles:

5 Display the cards around the room and, once again, check meaning and pronunciation.

Follow-up 1

Remind the learners of the cards at every available opportunity. For example, when a learner answers a question with a shrug, or with an expression in their mother tongue, point to the sign that says *I don't know*. The idea is that the expressions should become automatic responses to a variety of common classroom situations.

Follow-up 2

At periodic points in the course, repeat the activity with new expressions. The chunks that the class uses regularly and fluently can be replaced with the new ones.

Example

Let me think.
Wait a minute.
What's the answer [to number 1]?
That's not right.
I don't agree.
I got it right/wrong.
I haven't done it.
It's on page …
Let me see.
I don't remember.
What do you think?
Do you agree?
Whose turn is it?
Let's look it up.
Let's do it again.
Why not?
What for?

Comments:

There are grounds to believe that many learners go through a 'chunk learning' phase in advance of learning and applying grammar rules. Moreover, the chunks that they learn may become 'unpacked', over time, to 'release their grammar'. That is, the learner memorizes an expression like *I don't know* which is first used as if it were a single word. Only later is the chunk analysed into its component grammar structures, so that the learner is able to create *I don't understand*, or *I know*, or *You don't know*. It is important, therefore, that these chunks are taught at a very early stage, and well in advance of the point in the syllabus where the relevant grammar is first presented. There is no problem, in other words, in teaching *I haven't done it* long in advance of the first presentation of the **present perfect**, so long as it is taught 'as an expression', and that it is clearly associated with the typical situations in which it is used.

1.13 Grammar word families

Level Any

Time 20–30 minutes

Aims **To draw attention to the different grammar inflexions in English (i.e. the way grammar words are changed by the addition of different endings).**

Procedure

1 Draw a grid, like the one shown, on the board and ask learners to copy it. There should be as many columns as words you plan to dictate:

2 Dictate some common words, which learners copy into the first row of the grid, for example *work*, *may*, *be*, *had*, *went*, *must*, *written*, *good*, *put*, and *hot*. Check that these have been correctly spelt by eliciting the words back from the class, and writing them into the grid on the board.

3 Learners work in pairs or small groups to write as many grammatical forms of each word as they can think of. Give an example *work, works, working, worked*. Point out that, for the purposes of the activity, the forms should be grammatical, not **lexical**. Thus, while *worker* is a perfectly acceptable derivation of *work*, it doesn't have a grammatical function.

4 Individuals from each group or pair then come up to the board and fill in a column each. They should be challenged to identify the different forms, for example, *works* = present, third person singular; *better* = **comparative**.

Variation

This could be turned into a race, in which the winner is the group who produce the most correct entries in a given time limit (say five minutes).

Follow-up

In their same groups, learners use each of the word forms to write sentences which clearly display the use of the form. That means not simply *He works*, but *He works from nine to five every day*, for example.

Comments

This activity draws attention to the fact that English (unlike highly inflected languages) does not have a huge variety of inflected forms, and that just a few forms do a large amount of work. Note also that some **grammar words**, like *must*, have no derived forms at all.

1.14 Inflexion grid

Level Beginner

Time 15–25 minutes

Aims To encourage learners to work out inflected forms from a text.

Preparation

Text that contains as many examples of a word's inflected forms as possible. Here, for example, is a dialogue with forms of the verb *to be* embedded:

A Where were you yesterday?
B What was yesterday?
A It was Tuesday.
B I was in the library. Ask Ruth and Janet. We were all in the library. And Derek, too.
A Ruth and Janet were in class. And Derek was at home.
B Oh.

Procedure

Ask learners to copy a grammar grid from the board. For example:

I _____	we _____
you _____	
he/she/it _____	they _____

Either write (or project) the prepared text on the board, read the text aloud, or provide printed copies of the text. (The form of delivery will depend in part on the level of difficulty of the text.) Learners read (or listen) and then attempt to fill out the grid. They should then compare in pairs. A further reading may be required before they have completed the table.

Volunteers can then come and fill in the table on the board.

Follow-up

Learners use the completed table to write a text (for example, another dialogue) that incorporates as many of the forms as possible, and as naturally as possible. Learners can then exchange texts and decide which reads the most naturally.

Comment

The words that you choose to include in the text can be **lexical verbs** (for example, *write*, *writes*, *writing*, *wrote*, *written*), **auxiliary verbs** (for example, *have*, *having*, *has*, *had*), or **adjectives** (for example, *hot*, *hotter*, *hottest*). Or the targeted item could be **possessive determiners** (*my*, *your*, *her*, *his*, *its*, etc.) or **possessive pronouns** (*mine*, *yours*, *hers*, *his*, etc.). If it is too difficult to include these in a single text, example sentences can be used instead. For example, here are some sentences that display the different possessive pronouns:

This is mine. It's got my name on it.
This is yours. It's got your name on it.
This is hers. It's got her name on it.
etc.

1.15 Two-way verb pattern translation

Level Intermediate to advanced

Time 20–35 minutes

Aims To draw attention to the way the choice of verb determines the choice of pattern that follows it, and to contrast these patterns with verb patterns in the learners' first language.

Preparation

Sentences for dictation, containing at least two contrasting **verb** patterns. It's important that the vocabulary in the sentences is familiar to the learners so that they are not distracted by unknown words. (See Worksheet 1.15 below.)

Procedure

1 Learners, working individually, do not write down each sentence, but instead translate them into their first language and write down the translation. They should also be invited to ask questions about the sentences to ensure that they understand them perfectly. Allow them to compare their sentences in pairs, and, again, to ask for clarification, if necessary.

2 Now, working together, they translate the sentences back into English. These can be written on to the board by volunteers from the different groups.

3 Read out the original sentences, comparing them with the re-translated versions on the board, and inviting comments about any differences. The differences may be superficial and may not represent errors, simply different interpretations of the original. However, there may also be sentences that are ill-formed. These should be corrected on the board. If the error relates to the syntactic pattern following the verb (for example, **I explained to them the plan.*), this would be a good opportunity to draw attention to the pattern. Making an explicit contrast with the way the structure is expressed in the learners' first language is often a useful way of doing this.

4 Ask learners to categorize the different verbs that they have been using, according to the pattern that they take. For example, if the focus has been on verbs that take *-ing* vs verbs that take *to*-infinitive, ask them to divide the verbs into the two groups.

5 Finally, ask them to use the different verbs—or some of them—to write sentences about themselves, some of which are true and some false. They then exchange sentences with their classmates and decide which sentences are true and which are false.

Worksheet 1.15

Reporting verbs
The librarian told us to be quiet.
The waiter suggested we try the fish.
My doctor advised me to eat less.
Can you recommend a good hotel?
I warned you to slow down.
The teacher explained the rule to the class.
I promised I would write.

***-ing* vs *to*-infinitive**
Do you like having guests?
I forgot to buy petrol.
She enjoys working from home.
She's trying to give up smoking.
It kept raining all day.
They expect to arrive tomorrow.

Verbs with one or two objects
Barry sent you an email.
I'll tell you a joke.
Can you introduce me to Tom?
Give the dog its food.
Bring the boss his mail.
I explained the plan to them.

Comments

1 This activity is suitable for any feature of grammar, but works particularly well with the kinds of syntactic features that are often realized very differently from one language to another, such as **verb complementation**. (Verb complementation is the pattern that follows, and is dictated by, the choice of verb. Some verbs, like *know*, are followed by *that*-**clauses**, for example. Others, like *want*, are followed by the *to*-infinitive.)

2 Because it involves translation, this activity may seem suitable only for monolingual classes, but in fact it is possible to do with multilingual classes as well—each learner translating into his or her own mother tongue and then back into English. But, of course, in a multilingual class it may not be possible for learners to work together on the task, and nor will it be feasible to do much in the way of cross-linguistic comparison if more than one language is represented, and if the teacher is not familiar with the languages in question.

2

Sentence grammar

Introduction

Sentence grammar is the traditional domain of most grammar teaching, and essentially comprises what is commonly known as 'sentence structure', or more technically as **syntax**. Syntax is concerned with the rules that determine the way words can be combined to make well formed sentences. Syntax explains why *My aunt's pen is on the table.* is well formed while **Aunt's my pen the table on is.* is not. (The asterisk denotes an ill-formed sentence.) But grammar is more than just producing well formed sentences. The sentences also have to make sense—that is, they have to express the meaning that the speaker or writer intends. Thus *My pen's aunt is on the table.* or *The table's aunt is on my pen.* are both well formed, technically speaking, but they are unlikely to be accurate representations of a speaker's meaning. Sentence grammar, then, is not simply concerned with putting *any* words in the right order, but with putting the *right* words in the right order. Therefore, tasks that work on sentence grammar (such as the ones in this Part 2) need to maintain a balance between a concern for correct *form* with a concern for *meaning* as well.

The main preoccupation of sentence grammar has always been with the *verb phrase*. (A **verb phrase** is a group of one or more **verbs**, as in *went, was going, might have gone.*) There are a number of reasons for the emphasis on verb phrases. For a start, a sentence without a verb (**My aunt's pen on the table.*) is not normally considered well formed. More importantly, the verb phrase gathers together a great deal of key information about states, actions, and processes, including the time of occurrence, the degree of likelihood, whether the situation is finished or not, and so on. Knowing how to construct verb phrases also involves knowing rules of **morphology**, that is, the way words can change their form to convey different grammatical distinctions, for example, from *is* to *was*, or from *work* to *working*. While English is not a heavily inflected language, there are still morphological rules that learners have to come to grips with and many of these are verb-related. These facts account for the heavy emphasis on verbs in the syllabuses of most language teaching courses. It also accounts for the fact that many of the activities in this Part 2 have features of the verb phrase as their focus. This does not mean to say, though, that they can't be adapted to other—equally problematic—areas of grammar, such as the **noun phrase**. (A noun phrase is a noun and its associated **articles**, **adjectives**, etc., as in *my aunt's pen*, *the table*.)

What follows, then, are a variety of activities that are aimed at developing the learners' ability to interpret and to construct well formed and meaningful sentences in English. Some of these activities involve the use of complete texts, rather than isolated sentences. That is because sentences are usually best understood in their context. But the focus is still on aspects of grammar *within* the sentence, not *beyond* it. For a focus on aspects of grammar that extend beyond the sentence, see Part 3.

2.1 Sort the sentences

Level Any

Time 20–30 minutes

Aims To highlight the differences between related structures, and to draw attention to their distinguishing features.

Preparation

Write a selection of sentences on to the strips of card or paper. Alternatively, print one page of well-spaced sentences, make as many copies of this page as there are groups of students, and then cut the pages into strips, one sentence per strip.

Example Here is a selection of **conditional** sentences:

1 *It wouldn't be so cold if you closed the windows.*
2 *I would have left earlier if I'd known it was so late.*
3 *We'll phone if we get lost.*
4 *If the restaurant is closed, I'll order a takeaway.*
5 *What would you have done if you had been on your own?*
6 *If the printer was working, I'd print you a copy.*
7 *Jean would've come first if she hadn't slipped.*
8 *The car will start if you let the engine warm up.*
9 *Would you carry on working if you didn't have to?*

Make as many sets as there are groups.

Procedure

1. Put the learners into pairs or small groups.
2. Distribute the sets of jumbled sentences to the learners and tell them to lay the sentences out on a flat surface.
3. Tell them to sort the sentences into groups. Depending on the level of the class, and their familiarity with the area of grammar that the sentences focus on, you may let them decide a) how many groups there are, b) how many sentences there are in each group, and c) what the principle of categorization should be. However, it's often better if the learners themselves make these decisions, and the extra

effort deciding amongst themselves what the categories are will help increase the degree of cognitive engagement in the task. For example, the sentences above could be separated into two groups: sentences 3, 4, and 8, on the one hand, and sentences 1, 2, 5, 6, 7 and 9, on the other. The distinction underlying this classification is that between *real* and *unreal* conditions. But a three-way division is of course possible, whereby the *unreal* conditions are further subdivided into those that refer to present or future time (1, 6, and 9), and those that refer to past time (2, 5, and 7). This three-way division will be familiar to many learners as the distinction between 'first', 'second', and 'third' **conditionals**.

4 When the sentences have been sorted, ask learners to report on, and justify, their groupings. Use this stage to focus on the grammar rules, by challenging learners to explain the differences in form and meaning between the different groupings.

Follow-up 1

Once learners have organized the sentences into groups, and justified their choice, challenge them to regroup them, according to different criteria.

Follow-up 2

Ask learners to create more sentences—preferably about themselves—for each of the patterns they have identified.

Follow-up 3

Ask them to choose one sentence from each of the groupings, and, for each one, to write a paragraph or dialogue that includes it.

Comments

It is important that the sentences you select are intelligible to the learners and that they don't include vocabulary that is likely to be unfamiliar to them. To be sure, they should be invited to check any unfamiliar words before they start the categorizing task. The point is that the *grammar* of the sentences is the focus of their attention, not the vocabulary. Likewise, the sentences—although stripped of their context—should not be so unusual, mutilated, or obscure that their probable contexts couldn't easily be recovered. That is to say, the *meaning* of the sentences should be easily retrievable.

This is one reason why invented sentences generally work better than authentic sentences (such as those taken from a corpus) in this kind of exercise. One possible source of sentences is the coursebook that learners are using, particularly the texts in the coursebook that learners are already familiar with. However, carefully selected concordance data could serve just as well, especially at higher levels. On the next page is a selection of sentences taken from the British National Corpus that focus on different *if*-constructions, the task being to sort them into first, second, or third conditional structures, and those that fit none of these categories (from *natural Grammar* by Scott Thornbury, Oxford University Press, 2004).

Example

a She could have killed me **if** she'd wanted to.
b **If** it fitted in with a family holiday, then I might go.
c **If** I could just use the phone, I'll get a taxi.
d Wouldn't Mummy have been horrified **if** she'd known?
e **If** I've cooked it you'll eat it.
f **If** customers think products are too expensive, they will go elsewhere.
g The risk is even higher **if** you smoke and drink heavily.
h **If** you go back to sleep you won't have time to have breakfast.
i I am sure none of my clients would take me seriously **if** I didn't turn up in a sharp suit.
j **If** I am going to buy a plane, how much will it cost me?
k I think I could have done better **if** I had a different attitude.
l **If** it hadn't rained the night before, there could have been a major forest fire.
m You have to correct it **if** it is wrong.
n I reckon I could sleep **if** I was warm enough.

(S. Thornbury. *Natural Grammar*. Oxford University Press, 2004)

Concordance data such as this are available on the Internet (see Further Reading on page 128).

2.2 Minimal Sentence Pairs

Level Elementary and above

Time 20–30 minutes

Aims To focus attention on a structure by contrasting it with a related one; or to fine-tune learners' understanding of two related—and easily confused—structures.

Preparation

1 Prepare two sentences that are different in one grammatical particular. Sentences that contrast two **tenses**, or a simple vs a **continuous** form, or two different **modal verbs**, work well. Learners should be able to construct a plausible situation for each of the sentences without too much trouble. You should also keep the vocabulary within the learners' level of understanding, wherever possible so that their attention is focused on solving the 'grammar puzzle'.

Example

A 1 *She read a book last night.*
OR
2 *She was reading a book last night.*

B 1 *Has anyone phoned this morning?*
2 *Did anyone phone this morning?*

C 1 *Ed should've taken the umbrella.*
OR
2 *Ed must've taken the umbrella.*

D 1 *I liked the Volvo so I bought one.*
OR
2 *I liked the Volvo so I bought it.*

E 1 *How's your father—He's a little better.*
OR
2 *How's your father?—He's little better.*

F 1 *My brother, who lives in Rotterdam, is a lawyer.*
OR
2 *My brother who lives in Rotterdam is a lawyer.*

2 Prepare concept questions for the two sentences. These help to pin down the conceptual differences between the sentences. For the pair of sentences A, above, the concept questions might be:

She read a book last night. Did she finish the book? (Answer: *Yes*.)
She was reading a book last night. Did she finish the book? (Answer: *We don't know*.)

For sentence pair F, the concept questions might be:

My brother, who lives in Rotterdam, is a lawyer: How many brothers have I got? (Answer: *One, presumably*.)
My brother who lives in Rotterdam is a lawyer. How many brothers have I got? (Answer: *More than one*.)

Procedure

1 Write the two sentences on the board. Sort out any residual vocabulary problems that might hinder understanding of the sentences.

2 Ask learners to discuss in pairs or small groups the difference in a) the form, and b) the meaning, of the two sentences in the pair that you have written on the board.

3 Conduct an open class discussion, soliciting ideas from the learners as to the differences between the sentences. Focus first on the formal features of the sentences. For example, for the pair B, above, the questioning sequence might aim to cover the following facts:

TEACHER What words are different?
STUDENT *Has* and *did*, and *phoned* and *phone*.
TEACHER What do we call these two verb forms?
STUDENT In sentence 1 it is the present perfect, and in sentence 2 it is the past simple.

TEACHER How do you form each one?
STUDENT The present perfect is formed by the auxiliary verb *have* and the past participle of the verb. The regular past simple is formed by adding *-ed* to the verb. The question is formed by using *did* …, etc.

4 Next, focus on the differences of meaning that are expressed in the two sentences. This is where reference will need to be made to the extended context. For example, in pair B, you will need to establish the likely time frame within which the question was asked. For sentence 1 (*Has anyone phoned this morning?*) it is still the morning, whereas in sentence 2 (*Did anyone phone this morning?*) it is now the afternoon. To establish these facts, ask concept questions (see Preparation 2).

5 If necessary, extend the context in order to clarify the difference. For example, in pair C above, elicit continuations of each sentence, beginning *because* …:

1 *Ed should've taken the umbrella* because it's raining now, and he'll get wet without it.
2 *Ed must've taken the umbrella* because it's not here, and no one else took it.

Or, supply continuations, and ask the learners to match them with the sentence. For example, in pair E above, which sentence elicits the response: *I'm glad to hear it.* and which sentence elicits the response: *I'm sorry to hear it?* (Answer: *1 and 2, respectively.*)

6 Summarize the discussion by establishing a general rule or principle. For example, (sentence pair A): *We use the past simple to talk about past situations as a whole, from start to finish. We use the past continuous to talk about situations that were in progress at some time in the past, and are not necessarily finished, for example because they were interrupted.*

For sentence pair D, the summary might be: *We use one to mean 'a member of the group of things just mentioned'; we use it to refer to the specific thing just mentioned.*

Follow-up

Test learners' understanding of the difference between sentences through an exercise where they have to choose between the two contrasted forms.

Example Choose the best answer:

1 I *watched/was watching* television last night when Jill phoned.
2 I *watched/was watching* television last night and then I went to bed.
3 etc.

Variation 1

A variant using three or more sentences is called *Odd one out*. In this case, learners have to choose the sentence that doesn't fit in the set, and explain why. For example, what is the odd one out in this set?

1 *I hadn't met her before.*
2 *We had the kitchen painted.*
3 *Had it been raining when you arrived?*
4 *Where had I left my keys?*
5 *When we got there, the film had already started.*

(The odd one out is sentence 2, since it is an example of the 'causative *have*' (*to have something done*) while the others are all examples of the past perfect (*had done* or *had been doing*).)

Variation 2

A similar variant is called *Same or different?* Learners have to decide whether the two sentences in a pair have more or less the same meaning, or if they have a very different meaning.

Example In each pair, are the sentences more or less the same, or very different?

1 *It started to rain while we were changing the tyre.*
2 *It started raining while we were changing the tyre.*

3 *She stopped to tell me about her holiday.*
4 *She stopped telling me about her holiday.*

5 *He remembered to switch the lights out.*
6 *He remembered switching the lights out.*

7 *I like to have my teeth checked regularly.*
8 *I like having my teeth checked regularly.*

9 *I'd hate to have nothing to do.*
10 *I'd hate having nothing to do.*

(In these examples, sentences 1 and 2, and sentences 9 and 10, are more or less the same in meaning; the others are different.)

Variation 3

Learners have to supply the context for each of two similar sentences. So, for these two sentences, they have to include each one in a short (4 to 6 sentence) text:

a *He remembered to switch the lights out.*
b *He remembered switching the lights out.*

Here are some example contexts:

a James was the last person to leave the office. There were a number of things he had to do. *He remembered to switch the lights out.* But he forgot to close all the windows.
b After the robbery, the police asked James some questions. Unfortunately, he couldn't remember everything very clearly. *He remembered switching the lights out.* But he wasn't sure if he had closed all the windows.

Variation 4

The same principle as in Variation 3 can be used to design an activity where learners have to choose which sentence goes into a context.

Example Put each of these sentences into the correct place in either text 1 or text 2:

a *I would've.*
b *I should've.*

1 I'm sorry I didn't wash the car. It was me who got it all dirty. I promise I'll wash it next time.

2 I didn't wash the car. But I couldn't find anything to wash it with. Anyway, it wasn't very dirty.

Answers
Sentence (a) fits best in Text 2, after ... *the car.*
Sentence (b) fits best in Text 1, after ... *the car.*

Comments

In using decontextualized sentences, there is always a danger that learners lack sufficient information to be able to make a reasonable inference. This technique works best, therefore, where learners are *already* familiar with the target structures, but are still having problems choosing between the two. This familiarity may be based on previous exposure to the structures, or it may be based on knowledge of related structures. For example, in the following sentence pair learners' knowledge of the difference between the *present* simple and continuous may help them in working out the difference between the *past* simple and continuous:

1 *She read a book last night.*
2 *She was reading a book last night.*

2.3 True or false?

Level Any

Time 20–30 minutes

Aims To rehearse a grammar item in a personalized context.

Preparation

Prepare, for dictation, five or six sentences about yourself or about someone likely to be well known to the learners. Some of the sentences should be true, some false. At least one of the sentences should contain an item of grammar that you plan to highlight. For example, here are five sentences about the author of this book, one of which is false. They have been designed to include different time expressions (*since I was 25; never*) but could equally well be used to focus on a **verb** form, such as the **present perfect**:

I have been teaching since I was 25.
When I was 26 I went and taught in Egypt.
After that I taught in Poland for five years.
I once worked in New Zealand.
I have never taught in China or Japan.

Procedure

1 Tell the class you are going to dictate some sentences. At this stage, do not tell them who they are about, or that some are true and some false. Dictate the sentences, one at a time, at natural speed, repeating once or twice.

2 Allow learners to compare in pairs to make sure they have the same sentences. If there are any problems, dictate the problem sentences again.

3 Ask questions to check that learners know the meaning of any words that might be unfamiliar.

4 Ask individuals to read back the sentences aloud to the class, and/or ask learners to come and write the sentences on the board. It is very important, for the purposes of this activity, that the sentences are 'standardized', that is, that everyone has the same version.

5 Tell the class who the sentences are about (if they can't already guess), and tell them that some of the sentences are true, and some false. (You can choose whether or not to tell them how many are false.) Ask them to decide which are true and which are false, and to compare in pairs.

6 Have a show of hands about each sentence, challenging learners to justify their choice. Finally, tell the class the correct answer.

7 If the sentences are about yourself, invite the learners to ask more questions about any of the topics mentioned. For example, *Why did you go and teach in Egypt? Would you like to work in China or Japan?*, etc.

8 Now it is time to focus on the embedded language feature. For example, each of the following sentences has a time **adverbial** embedded in it. (A time **adverbial** is a word, **phrase**, or **clause** which adds information about time to the sentence.)

I have been teaching ***since I was 25****.*
When I was 26 *I went and taught in Egypt.*
After that *I taught in Poland* ***for five years****.*
I ***once*** *worked in New Zealand.*
I have ***never*** *taught in China or Japan.*

Show learners one example of the targeted feature, then ask them to find the same feature in the other sentences.

9 Conduct an open class feedback on the task, using this opportunity to ask questions aimed at drawing attention to relevant grammar rules—such as the use of *for* with periods of time (*for five years*) and *since* with the point of time at which an activity began (*since I was 25*)—or the use of the **present perfect** to talk about situations that started in the past and extend to the present, and the use of the **past simple** to talk about situations that are separated from the present.

10 Ask the learners individually to write sentences that are true about themselves, using the targeted grammar feature or features. (This could also be turned into a true/false activity, with learners asked to include some 'misinformation' in their sentences.)

11 Learners then form small groups to take turns to read their sentences aloud to one another and say if they think the sentences are true or false, if this option in Stage 11 has been chosen. Learners then use these sentences as the basis for a conversation in which they ask further questions about the content of each other's sentences.

Variation 1

The same process can be used to contrast two related structures, as in Activity 2.2. For example, the sentences chosen above could be used to focus on the difference between the present perfect and the past simple. In this case, learners can be asked first to separate the sentences into two groups.

Variation 2

1 Having dictated your own sentences (as in Stages 1–7 above), omit the language focus (Stage 8) but instead ask learners to create sentences about themselves, using your sentences as a model, and to write these down. Learners should use your sentences as a model but no grammar point is preselected.

2 Elicit some of these back on to the board, and group them according to the language structures they embed. For example, put all the sentences that use the present perfect together, and all the sentences that use the past simple together—or all the sentences that use *for* and all the sentences that use *since*.

3 Elicit corrections for any sentences that are not well formed.

4 Use these sentences as the 'data' for the language focus, as in Stage 8 above.

Comments

1 Dictating the sentences in Stages 1–4 ensures that learners engage with both the form and the meaning of the sentences but you could also simply write the sentences on the board for learners to copy down. Then proceed as in Stage 5.

2 Other topics which could be used are daily routine, free-time activities, the school curriculum, or even last night's TV viewing, all of which provide content for this kind of activity, as well as providing useful models for the learners' own sentences. Here are some examples (with time adverbials underlined):

My sister phoned ***while I was having dinner.***
I forgot to feed the cat ***this morning.***
This time next week *I'll be on holiday.*
Yesterday evening *I took the dog for a walk.*
etc.

2.4 Grammaticality judgements

Level Any

Time 20–30 minutes

Aims To encourage learners to reflect on common errors; to assess learners' intuition about grammar.

Preparation

Prepare a worksheet with a list of sentences, some of which are well formed, and others which are not. It is a good idea to base these on the learners' own sentences: you can collect these from their homework, from class work, or from regular tests.

Example Worksheet 2.4a is based on sentences produced by a group of elementary students, in response to the question *What do you like doing in your free time?*

> **Worksheet 2.4a**
>
> What do you like doing in your free time?
>
> 1 I like playing the violin.
> 2 All my free time I am with my baby. She likes look books and play games.
> 3 I spend my free time listening music.
> 4 I don't have a lot of free time.
> 5 I spend my free time working with my dog called Frida.
> 6 I quite enjoy surfing the Internet.
> 7 We go to swimming pool because we like to swimming too much.
> 8 I like to play tennis in my free time.
> 9 I'm a student. So I have no enough time for entertainments.
> 10 I spend my free time going to a walk with my friends.

Worksheet 2.4b was used with a group of upper-intermediate students, and was based on sentences in compositions they had written on the topic of relationships.

Worksheet 2.4b

Relationships

1 I think he was attracted to me.
2 A friend of mine was going to a party and asked me if I would like to come.
3 I knew him since I was a child.
4 He has had a lot of experience of the life.
5 I have a friend who I think she is very sociable.
6 I explained my feelings to him.
7 I didn't like very much his behaviour.
8 He told me that he had always wanted to meet me.
9 I think is very important that workmates get on well together.
10 Next December he and I are going to get married.
11 His behaviour repels me.
12 I explained him why I felt angry with him.

Procedure

1 Hand out the worksheet and ask learners, working in pairs or small groups, to decide which of the sentences are well formed and which are not. Those that are not, they should attempt to correct. (You can make the task slightly easier by telling them how many of the sentences are correct.)

2 Ask learners to volunteer their opinions in open class. Correct the incorrect sentences, and elicit the rule underlying each correction.

Variation 1

1 Hand the worksheet out, as above, but before students work in pairs or small groups, have them work individually. Set a time limit, for example, a minute, for a quick 'skim through' in which learners have to mark the sentences right or wrong, keeping a note of these initial judgements. They then work in pairs or groups for a less hurried evaluation of the sentences.

2 As in Step 2 above, conduct open class feedback and correct the incorrect sentences.

3 Ask learners to compare their initial judgements with the final answers. Often, first impressions are the best ones—or, at least, they reveal more about a learner's intuitions than do judgements made after lengthy deliberation.

Variation 2

1 Hand the worksheet out. Use the sentences as a basis for a game (called *Grammar auction*). Organize the class into a minimum of three groups.

2 Each group is allotted a fixed sum of 'money' to start with—for example, $5000.

3 Take the role of the auctioneer yourself, and 'auction' the sentences one by one, saying, for example, *How much am I offered for this sentence? $100? $200?* etc.

4 The groups bid against each other for the sentences. The idea is to 'buy' only correct sentences. The group who bids most, gets to 'own' the sentence. Keep a record of how much each group has spent.

5 At the end of the bidding, go back over the sentences, pointing out which ones are correct and which are not, and why.

6 The group who—at the end of the game—has the most correct sentences *and* the most money left over, is the winner.

Acknowledgements

The Grammar auction idea comes from *Grammar Games*, by Mario Rinvolucri, Cambridge University Press, 1984.

Substitution activities

Substitution tables were associated with audiolingualism, a teaching method used in the 1950s and 1960s. Audiolingualism fell out of favour when behaviourism, its theoretical basis, became discredited. Consequently, many of the activities associated with audiolingualism were abandoned, including the use of substitution tables. However, substitution tables can be an excellent way of displaying grammar structures. Activities 2.5–2.9 below exploit the cognitive potential of these tables.

2.5 The sentence-making machine

Level Any

Time 15–30 minutes

Aims To demonstrate and exploit the generative power of substitution tables.

Preparation

Select a grammar pattern and design a substitution table that displays it, for example:

I [name] and I [name] and [name] My brother/sister, etc. and I	have	**got**	a/an	pet	fish rat dog
[name] Our family My brother My sister My best friend Someone I know No one I know motorbike watch	has			[brand name]	skateboard snowboard laptop digital camera mobile phone stereo bike

Another example of a grammar pattern substitution table:

I've	[never]	seen been to eaten worked in touched met	a kangaroo a crocodile a comet Australia a pineapple London a foreign country shark-fin soup a ghost the President a unicorn	[once.] [more than once.] [many times.]

(S. Thornbury. *Highlight Pre-Intermediate Student's Book.* Heinemann, 1994)

Procedure

1 Present the table on the board, on a large sheet of paper, or by means of a projector.

2 Demonstrate how the table works by constructing two or three sentences yourself, pointing (ideally with a pointer) at the relevant part of the table as you say the sentences. For the purposes of this game, only affirmative sentences should be made. For example:

Kees has got a Seiko watch.
Someone I know has got a pet snake.

3 Put the learners into pairs or small groups, and ask them to make as many true sentences as they can. You can add a competitive element by setting a time limit: the student or group that produces the most well formed *true* sentences is the winner. This will involve them justifying the truth of their sentences, for example by giving more information about the situation they have described.

Variation 1

Present a table and ask learners to see *how many* well formed, plausible sentences they can generate from it, for example:

Joanna We I Karen and Tony	walk drives play watches	TV. to school. home. tennis.

(This table generates thirteen sentences.)

Variation 2

1 Using an overhead or data projector, or a large sheet of paper, display a table briefly—30 second at most.

2 The learners, working in pairs or groups, see how many sentences they can construct from memory. They write these down.

3 When they have run out of ideas, or on expiry of a time limit, display the table again. The learners read out their sentences and these are checked against the table. The team with the most correct sentences are the winners. Here is a table that works well for this activity with pre-intermediate students:

What	do you does he	like dislike	doing?	
I		like don't like enjoy	watching playing	football. tennis.
He		likes hates	wearing	jeans. pyjamas.

I	can't stand don't mind	people who	complain in restaurants. smoke in the street.

(B. Abbs et al. *Building Strategies*. Longman, 1975)

Variation 3

1 Using a substitution table that all the learners can see, read sentences to the class, some of which are well formed, others of which are not. They have to evaluate the sentences according to the evidence of the substitution table. The following sentences are based on the *Strategies* table above:

I like watching football.
**He don't like playing tennis.*
**I don't mind people who wearing jeans.*
What does he dislike doing?
**I likes wearing pyjamas.*
etc.

2 Once the learners have got the idea, they can do the same in pairs, taking turns to generate and 'test' sentences on their partner.

2.6 Substitution jigsaw

Level Any

Time 10–20 minutes

Aims To focus attention on grammatical forms.

Materials Adhesive (such as Blu-tack™) to attach word cards to the board.

Preparation

Use a set of filing cards. On each card is written one word or phrase that constitutes one element in a substitution table. For example, the following twenty-one cards are derived from the table that is displayed beneath them. All the cards should be the same size. (If the cards are written in upper case, there are fewer non-grammatical clues as to the order in which they should go. This way, the learners' attention is focused solely on the grammar.)

WATCHING TV	LATELY	HAVE	THE DOGS	ALL WEEK
FEELING UNWELL	LIVING TOGETHER	DIANA	DRIVING	HAS
SINCE 1997	FOR 3 HOURS	MY FRIEND AND I	ALL NIGHT	I
BEEN	HE	WORKING	SINCE MIDDAY	YOU AND SUE
BARKING				

DIANA	HAS	BEEN	WORKING	ALL WEEK
HE			DRIVING	FOR 3 HOURS
YOU AND SUE	HAVE		WATCHING TV	SINCE MIDDAY
MY FRIEND AND I			LIVING TOGETHER	SINCE 1997
THE DOGS			BARKING	ALL NIGHT
I			FEELING UNWELL	LATELY

Procedure

1 Hand individual cards to class members, plus adhesive, one at a time. Their job is to come up and place them on the board in such a way as to form a coherent substitution table. Initially, it will not be clear what structure the table displays, but as more cards are placed on the board, learners should start to see a pattern and arrange them accordingly.

2 Continue handing out the cards until all the cards have been placed in their correct columns on the board.

3 Elicit some example sentences from the table, to show how it works.

Variation

Make enough sets of the cards for the learners to work in pairs or small groups. They arrange the cards on a flat surface to form the substitution table.

2.7 Variable substitution drill

Level Any

Time 5–10 minutes

Aims To encourage rapid, 'on-line' processing of sentence patterns.

Preparation

Plan a 'model' sentence and a series of 'prompts' designed to trigger manipulations of the sentence. These can be written out in sequence, or in the form of a substitution table.

Example

Model sentence: I've been here since five o'clock.

PROMPT 1	*six*
RESPONSE	I've been here since six o'clock.
PROMPT 2	*five hours*
RESPONSE	I've been here for five hours.
PROMPT 3	*five days*
RESPONSE	I've been here for five days.
PROMPT 4	*Tuesday*
RESPONSE	I've been here since Tuesday.
PROMPT 5	*She*
RESPONSE	She's been here since Tuesday.
PROMPT 6	*They*
RESPONSE	They've been here since Tuesday.
PROMPT 7	*last week*
RESPONSE	They've been here since last week.
PROMPT 8	*two weeks*
RESPONSE	They've been here for two weeks.

etc.

Procedure

1 Say the model sentence a number of times, slowing it down and speeding it up so that learners can hear the different words which make it up.

2 With a gesture, get learners to repeat the whole sentence in chorus.

3 Ask individuals to repeat the sentence.

4 Give the first prompt. Select one or two individuals, in turn, to modify the original sentence, incorporating the prompt.

5 Give the second prompt, and continue in this fashion, until the prompts have all been used.

Follow-up

In pairs, learners can take turns to give the prompts, and to respond to one another, using a substitution table as a guide.

2.8 Cut-up questions

Level Any

Time 20–30 minutes

Aims To draw attention to the word order, and use of auxiliaries, in questions.

Preparation

Use a set of word cards, each card about half the size of a normal visiting card. Write a selection of short questions on the cards, one word or phrase per card. Ideally the questions should consist of an equal number of words or phrases, and be notionally or thematically related. It helps, too, if the cards are all the same size. Use capital letters, so that there are no punctuation clues as to the word order. For the same reason, on separate, smaller cards, prepare as many question marks as there are questions.

Example Here is a set of four four-word questions, suitable for an elementary group:

WHEN	WERE	YOU	BORN	?
WHAT	IS	YOUR	JOB	?
WHERE	DID	YOU	STUDY	?
WHO	WAS	YOUR	TEACHER	?

Here is a set of cards that mix passive and active sentences, more suitable for an intermediate group:

WAS	YOUR	CAR	STOLEN	?
DID	YOU	LOCK	IT	?
HAVE	YOU	REPORTED	THE THEFT	?
HAS	ANYONE	BEEN	ARRESTED	?

There should be enough packs of these cards for each group of three to four learners. Shuffle the cards in each pack so that the questions are no longer in order.

Procedure

1 Distribute the sets of cards to the learners, working in groups of three or four. Ideally, they should be able to spread them out, face up, on a flat surface. Tell them to sort the cards into questions, indicating the number of questions that there are (for example, four) and the number of cards that comprise each question, if the questions are of equal length. Point out, too, that there should be no cards left unused.

2 Monitor the groups as they work, indicating—if appropriate—any ill-formed combinations.

3 When most of the groups seem to have finished, elicit the correct combinations on to the board.

4 Ask the class to tell you the rules of formation in each case. This may mean first asking them to group the sentences into categories, for example, *active* and *passive*. Elicit the rules of formation for each category.

Variation 1

To make the task easier, write the answers to the questions on the board. For the first set of questions (above), the answers might be:

In 1976.
I'm an archaeologist.
Dr Janet Wills.
At the University of Leicester.

Variation 2

Script a short dialogue that includes the questions that have been cut up, and record it (for example, with a colleague). For example, for the first set of questions above, the dialogue might be:

A Can I just ask you a few questions?
B Of course.
A First of all, when were you born?
B In 1983.
A I see. And where did you study?
B University, you mean?
A Yes.
B In Aberdeen.

A And what do you do now?
B I'm a systems analyst.
A I see. Who was your teacher?
B Terry McKenzie.
A: OK, that's all I need to know. Thanks.

When learners have had a first attempt at sorting the cards, play them the recording, as many times as necessary, so that they can check and modify the order of their cards.

Alternatively, having ordered the cards, the learners can write their own dialogues that incorporate the questions.

Comments

Of course, any sentences—not just questions—can be used like this. But because of the changes in word order involved in question formation in English, questions are particularly suitable for an ordering exercise. Indirect (or reported) questions, such as *Can you tell me where the bus leaves from?* also lend themselves to this treatment.

The task is harder than it looks. Depending on the selection of questions, there may be some correct (i.e. well formed) questions that have to be rejected, because otherwise there would be cards left unused. For example, using the first set of questions above, the learners might organize them—initially—like this:

WHERE WERE YOU BORN?
WHAT DID YOU STUDY?
WHO WAS YOUR TEACHER?

But this will mean that the remaining words are unusable: WHEN, IS, YOUR, JOB. It's important that learners know, however, which questions are acceptable and which are not—this can be dealt with at stage 3 in the procedure above, by asking, 'Did you form any other questions that you think are correct?'

2.9 One of us ... two of us ...

Level Any
Time 10–20 minutes
Aims To provide personalized review of a grammar structure.

Procedure

1 Write the following rubric on the board:

One of us can
Two of us
Three of us
None of us

2 Explain that '... of us' means 'of our group' and that 'none' means 'not one'. Elicit ways of completing the pattern. For example, 'One of us can drive. None of us can speak Russian.'

3 Divide the class into groups of four. Give them a rough time limit—say ten minutes—within which they must try and generate as many true sentences as they can about their group, using the rubric. One member of the group should be appointed to write down the sentences that are generated.

4 Ask the group 'secretaries' to read out some of the more interesting sentences about their group, and use this as an opportunity to draw out the students, inviting them to tell the class a little more about the things they have said they can do.

Comments

The activity can, of course, be adapted to any structure. For example:

has/have got
has/have (ever)
is/are going to
used to
would (ever)

Acknowledgements

Mario Rinvolucri first brought this highly productive activity to my attention.

2.10 Personalize the exercise

Level Any

Time 15–25 minutes

Aims To make a grammar exercise more memorable by personalizing it.

Preparation

Use any grammar exercise that consists of sentences, from any coursebook, workbook, or grammar practice book.

Example The following exercise comes from a grammar practice book:

Rewrite the sentences with *may*.

▸ Perhaps Sarah's ill. *Sarah may be ill.*
▸ Perhaps we'll go out. *We may go out.*
1 Perhaps it won't rain. ____
2 Perhaps we'll buy a car. ____
3 Perhaps Joe is not at home. ____
4 Perhaps Ann needs help. ____
5 Perhaps the baby's hungry. ____
6 Perhaps I won't change my job. ____
7 Perhaps she's married. ____
8 Perhaps he doesn't want to talk to you. ____

(Michael Swan and Catherine Walter. *The Good Grammar Book*. Oxford University Press, 2001)

Procedure

1 Hand out the exercise, or refer learners to the relevant exercise in their books.

2 Use the example sentences (for example, *Perhaps Sarah's ill.*) to elicit a personalized example, substituting *Sarah* for the name of one of the learners—preferably one who might in fact be ill! Ask them to work in pairs to continue adapting the sentences so that they give some local reference.

3 The pairs can then exchange sentences and complete the exercise.

Comments

This idea obviously works best on sentences that are about people, where names and relationships can be changed to represent people familiar to the learners.

Variation

Another way of 'personalizing' grammar exercises is to design them so that the sentences of the exercise become the stimulus for a follow-up speaking activity.

Example The following exercise is designed first to test learners' grasp of the form of the second **conditional**:

Choose the correct form of the verb to complete these sentences:

1 If public transport *is/was* free, people *will/would* stop driving cars.
2 If everyone *is/was* paid the same, no one *will/would* work hard.
3 It *will/would* be better if everyone *spoke/speaks* the same language.
4 If TV *is/was* more educational, nobody *will/would* watch it.
5 It [*will/would*] be nice if it [*is/was*] summer all the time.
6 If people [*can/could*] choose the sex of their babies, there [*will/would*] be more boys than girls.

After the learners have done the exercise, and you have checked it, ask them to form pairs or small groups and discuss whether, and why, they agree or disagree with the sentences.

2.11 Guess the sentence

Level Intermediate and above

Time 10–20 minutes

Aims To review grammar structures.

Preparation

Choose a sentence of about 8–10 words. The following examples all come from a coursebook unit.

Spain is famous for its unusual lifestyle.
She always drinks fifteen glasses of water a day.
Can I pay by credit card?

The important thing is that the sentences should be ones that your learners have encountered recently in class.

Procedure

1 Tell the class that they have to guess what the sentence is by asking **yes/no questions** about each word. Provide some sample questions on the board, for example:

Is the first word 'the'?
Is the second word a noun?
Does it begin with G?
Is the verb in the past tense?
Has it got two syllables?

2 When the class have worked out the sentence, put them into pairs or small groups to do the same. Each learner should secretly choose a sentence from their notebook or coursebook—preferably one that has occurred recently—and the others take turns to guess it.

Variation

Sentence hangman. The word game, *hangman*, can be adapted for the purposes of making the above activity more competitive. Each wrong guess of a word results in one element of the hangman being drawn on a piece of paper. If the sentence has not been fully guessed by the time the hanged man is drawn, the person guessing loses. Since this effectively allows learners only eleven wrong guesses, it is important that the sentence should come from a limited pool of possible sentences, for example, only sentences from the last lesson, or even—if played at the end of class—from the immediate lesson.

2.12 Picasso sentences

Level Elementary and above

Time 20–30 minutes

Aims To review any grammar structure.

Preparation

Prepare about six to eight sentences which include the target structure, and which represent a situation that can be drawn. Write the sentences on slips of paper.

Example Here are six sentences that practise the **present perfect** with *just*:

My sister has just had a baby.
My uncle has just been to New York.
My grandparents have just moved house.
My elder brother has just had an operation.
My younger brother has just graduated.
My daughter has just learnt to read.

Procedure

1 Demonstrate the activity: attempt to elicit a sentence that contains the structure you have selected by drawing on the board. This will be easier if it is a structure that has been recently presented and practised. For example, to elicit the sentence *My parents have just been to Egypt*, draw two stick figures on the board, and shapes to represent the Pyramids. Write a recent date above the picture. Draw further stick figures, if necessary, to establish the relationship (i.e. parents) with yourself. Once learners have more or less guessed the sentence, tidy it up for them, and then write it on the board—this will serve as a model.

2 Divide the class into teams of about three or four students each. Each member of each team will take turns to come to the front of the class, be shown one of the sentences (all team representatives are shown the same sentence simultaneously), and return to their group where they 'draw' the sentence. Speaking, writing, or mime are not allowed.

3 The first group to produce the full sentence aloud and correctly formed, according to the model, wins a point. Then another team representative comes forward from each group, and the process is repeated with a new sentence.

4 When all the sentences have been used, elicit the sentences back from the groups and write them on the board (their drawings will help to remind them of what the sentences were about). Use this stage to focus on the form and meaning of the structure.

2.13 Sentence race

Level Pre-intermediate and above

Time 5–10 minutes

Aims To play with the constraints imposed by word order.

Procedure

1 Divide the class into two teams, and divide the board into two halves by drawing a vertical line down the middle. In the top left-hand corner of each half of the board write the same word. It should be a word that typically begins a sentence, for example, for lower levels *The, A, Yesterday* … or, for higher levels *If, Although, Having, Before* … etc. Hand a board pen (or piece of chalk) to one member of each team. They are now ready to begin the 'race'.

2 The object of the game is to produce, in a time limit (say, two minutes), the longest correct sentence that begins with the pre-selected word. A member of each team adds one word at a time to the developing sentence, and then hands the board pen to another team member. If a word is incorrect (for example, because it doesn't agree with the word that precedes it, or if it is the wrong part of speech) the teacher simply erases it, without explanation. For example, if the

sentence on the board reads *Although I had not* ... and the next student adds *went* you erase this word without comment. If the next student adds *been*, this is acceptable. The only rule is that the sentences must be grammatically correct, and that 'lists' of more than two similar items are not permitted (in order to avoid the strategy of extending the sentence indefinitely by using a string of **adjectives**, for example.)

3 On expiry of the time limit, the last player is allowed to add a maximum of three words in order to complete the sentence. Then the number of words in each sentence is totalled, and the team with the most words wins.

Variation

To add an extra degree of challenge, teams are not allowed to repeat a word.

2.14 Disappearing sentences

Level Any

Time 5–15 minutes

Aims To encourage learners to internalize features of grammar.

Preparation

Select two or three long-ish sentences from texts that the learners have previously read or listened to, and which incorporate features of the grammar item you want to focus on.

Example The following sentences all come from the horoscope page of a women's magazine, and feature *will* to make predictions:

Don't worry as everything will sort itself out eventually.
You may well learn something that will help you in the future.
An open discussion will help both of you to come to a better understanding.
The important thing is to remember still to look after yourself so that you'll be there for others who rely on you.

(Russell Grant. 'What's in your stars?' *Woman's Weekly*. 2 November 2004)

Procedure

1 Write the complete sentences on the board. Ask an individual to read the first sentence aloud. Then erase one or two words from the sentence, replacing them with lines, for example:

Don't worry as everything _____ _____ *itself out eventually.*

Ask another learner to read the sentence, including the parts you have erased. Continue erasing sections of the sentence, substituting lines, and asking different learners to try and recall the complete sentence, until the whole sentence has been erased.

2 Do the same with the other sentences.

Variation

Instead of isolated sentences, you can also use a short text, but, again, it should be one that learners are already familiar with, such as a dialogue from their coursebook that they have both listened to and read previously (see also Activity 2.19 below).

Follow-up

Learners can do the same activity in pairs. They choose sentences of their own, from their coursebooks, and take turns to test one another's recall by progressively erasing (or blacking out) parts of the sentence.

Acknowledgements

This idea comes from Dave Willis's book *Rules, Patterns and Words*. Cambridge University Press, 2003.

2.15 Parsing

Level **Intermediate and above**

Time **20–30 minutes**

Aims **To develop learners' ability to parse sentences (i.e. to break sentences into their component parts).**

Materials **Cards and Blu-tack™.**

Preparation

1 Prepare enough cards so that each student has at least one. On each card write a word or phrase that might form a syntactic element of a sentence, such as a **subject**, **verb**, an **object**, a **complement**, or an **adverbial**. An example selection is given on the next page.

2 Also, prepare some complete sentences using similar words and phrases for dictation, or in the form of a handout, for example:

The old sailor told the children a story.
My uncle's new car is a Chrysler.
I went to Italy last summer.
The police arrested a man outside the bank.
It is very noisy in here.
Terry has lent me his new bike.
The children laughed at the clown.

3 Optionally, photocopy the grid on page 66, and provide a copy of it to each learner.

LAST NIGHT

JULIA

WAS READING

A BOOK

IN BED

YESTERDAY

MY FRIEND AND I

WERE

BUSY

AT SCHOOL

ON THURSDAY

OUR NEIGHBOURS

WERE ROBBED

AT WORK

AT FIVE O'CLOCK

THE TEACHER

GAVE

US

A LESSON

IN THE LIBRARY

Procedure

1 In advance, draw a grid on the board, like this:

Subject	Verb	Complement	Object (indirect) (direct)		Adverbial(s)	

2 Briefly explain that the grid represents the different parts of a sentence.

3 Distribute the cards, one to each learner.

4 The learners get up and walk around, reading one another's words and attempting to form sentences that make sense.

5 When most of them have managed to incorporate their word into a sentence, and thereby attach themselves to a group, ask them to come and stick their sentences on to the board, placing each card in the right place in the grid. It is likely that at first they will be unsure as to which categories the cards should go into (apart, perhaps, for **subject** and **verb**). At this stage, this is not important. If they are in doubt, simply show them. In the end the grid may look something like this:

Subject	Verb	Complement	Object (indirect) (direct)		Adverbial(s)	
Julia	was reading			a book	in bed	last night
My friend and I	were	busy			at school	yesterday
Our neighbours	were robbed				at work	on Thursday
The teacher	gave		us	a lesson	in the library	at five o'clock

Note that there are many other combinations that are possible. But for the purposes of demonstrating the sentence elements, the above combinations are sufficient.

6 Learners return to their seats. Now, explain the categories—or elicit explanations from the class. Put simply, the **subject** of the sentence is the actor or agent of an action or state; the action or state is expressed by the **verb**; the **object** is the recipient of the action, and

can be either direct or indirect, as in *Julia gave us a book*, where *a book* is the direct object, and *us* is the indirect object. The *complement* follows **verbs** like *is*, or *seems*, and tells us more about the subject. **Adverbials** usually provide circumstantial information, such as the time and place of the situation. Adverbials can often go in different places in the order of sentence elements—for example, at the beginning, as in *Last night Julia was reading a book in bed*. When they go at the end of the sentence, the usual order is *place* and then *time*—*Julia was reading a book in bed last night*. These five elements (abbreviated to S, V, O, C, A) are the essentials for understanding English **syntax**.

7 Dictate, or write on the board, or hand out, the sentences you have prepared. Ask learners to work in pairs to 'parse' the sentences, i.e. to identify their SVOCA elements.

8 Check their parsing by asking individuals to come and write a sentence each into the grid on the board, putting the elements in the correct place, for example:

Subject	**Verb**	**Complement**	**Object** (indirect)	(direct)	**Adverbial(s)**	
The old sailor	told		the children	a story.		
My uncle's new car	is	a Chrysler.				
I	went				to Italy	last summer.
The police	arrested			a man	outside the bank.	
It	is	very noisy			in here.	
Terry	has lent		me	his new bike.		
The children	laughed				at the clown.	

Alternatively, make copies of the blank grid, distribute them, and ask learners to write the sentence elements into the grid.

Follow-up 1

On the basis of the sentences that have been analysed so far, ask learners to decide what kinds of words, or **phrases**, typically go into each of the SVOCA 'slots'. For example, the **subject** is typically a **noun**, a **pronoun**, or a **noun phrase** (i.e. a **noun** and its accompanying **articles**, **adjectives**, etc.), as in *Julia, I, My uncle's new car*. As a guide, the following grid gives the more common ways that these sentence elements are realized:

Subject	Verb	Complement	Object	Adverbial(s)
noun	verb	noun	noun	prepositional phrase *(to work*, at *midday)*
noun phrase		noun phrase	noun phrase	adverb *(slowly, often)*
pronoun		*-ing* word	pronoun	adverb phrase *(very slowly)*
-ing word *(swimming)*			participle clause *(watching tennis)*	adverbial clause *(when I was five)*
wh-clause *(what I like)*			*that*-clause *(that I was hungry)*	

Follow-up 2

1 Write some sentence patterns on the board, for example:

SV
SVO
SVC
SVOO
SVA
SVOA

2 Check that learners understand the abbreviations.

3 Dictate some sentences, similar to the sentences used above (*Terry has lent me his new bike*, etc.). Ask learners to tell you which pattern each sentence is an example of. For example, *Terry has lent me his new bike* = SVOO.

4 Ask learners to create new sentences, one for each pattern.

Follow-up 3

1 Dictate, or write on the board, a selection of verbs that take different patterns of verb complementation (i.e. the sentence elements that follow the V slot) such as:

enjoy	*offer*	*behave*
suggest	*put*	*arrive*
disappear	*lose*	*explain*
seem	*greet*	*tell*
escape	*recommend*	*become*

2 Write some common patterns on the board, i.e. SV, SVO, SVC, SVOO, SVA, SVOA.

3 Ask learners to match the verbs with their patterns. Allow them to use dictionaries if necessary. Note that some verbs take more than one pattern. For example, *escape* can take the simple pattern SV, as in *the prisoner escaped*, and SVA: *the prisoner escaped from jail*. But in this second case, the A element is not obligatory. Compare that with *put*—*I put the milk in the fridge* (SVOA). Here both the O and the A elements are obligatory. The patterns commonly associated with the verbs in the list are:

enjoy	SVO *(We enjoyed the food. He doesn't enjoy looking after the children.)*
suggest	SVO *(I suggested a meal. She suggested that we have a break.)*
disappear	SV *(The plane disappeared.)*
seem	SVC *(The children seemed tired.)*
escape	SV *(The prisoner escaped.)*
offer	SVOO *(Ted offered me a sandwich.)*
put	SVOA *(I put the milk in the fridge.)*
lose	SVO *(She lost her passport.)*
greet	SVO *(They greeted the prime minister.)*
recommend	SVO *(I wouldn't recommend this restaurant.)*
behave	SVA *(The children were behaving badly.)*
arrive	SV *(Your taxi has arrived.); also* SVA *(We arrived on Friday.)*
explain	SVO *(The doctor explained the situation.); also* SVOA *(The doctor explained the situation to me.)*
tell	SVOO *(The teacher told the children a story.); also* SVO *(He told a rude joke.)*
become	SVC *(He became sad.)*

4 Ask learners to create their own sentences that display the pattern. Even better if these sentences are true sentences about themselves or people they know. They can then compare them, in pairs or in open class, and comment on them.

Comments

For lower-level learners, or learners who are totally new to this kind of grammar, you can simplify the grid you use, so that the headings look like this:

Subject	Verb	Object(s)/Complement	Adverbial(s)

For more information about verb patterns, see *Grammar Patterns 1: Verbs*, Collins COBUILD, 1996.

Acknowledgements

I am grateful to Ian Soper for these ideas. Ian works mainly with students from Asian language backgrounds whose problems in writing English often derive from a lack of understanding of how sentence elements are constructed and sequenced. These kinds of analytic tasks have proved to be very helpful.

2.16 Meaning through action

Level Beginner

Time 15–25 minutes

Aims To represent the meaning of a grammar structure through actions.

Procedure

1 Perform a set of actions in front of the class, at the same time providing a running commentary on the actions.

Example *I am walking to the door. The door is closed. What am I going to do? I'm going to open the door.*

Now, I am walking to the window. The window is open. What am I going to do? I am going to close the window.

Now, I am walking to the blackboard. I am holding the chalk. What am I going to do? I am going to write on the board.

2 Repeat the activities, but this time pause before the final sentence of each sequence, and elicit the answer to the question, for example you may say *What am I going to do?* to elicit *You are going to open the door.*

3 Ask individuals to perform the actions, while you provide the commentary: *Ahmed is walking to the window. What is he going to do?* etc.

4 Ask individuals to provide the commentary while first you, then another learner, perform the actions.

5 Display the structure on the board in the forms that have been used so far:

What	am I	going to	do?
	is he		

I	am	going to	open the door
you	are		close the window
he	is		write on the board

Comments

This activity arises out of the 'Direct Method', a core principle of which is that the new structure is associated with its meaning 'directly', i.e. unmediated by translation, explanation, etc. This works well for grammar structures that can be easily enacted, such as:

present continuous: *I am walking*
going to future: *I am going to open the door.*
imperatives: *Give me the book. Don't sit down.*
present perfect + *just: I have just closed the window.*
possessive determiners and **pronouns**: *This is my book. It is mine.*
demonstratives: *This book is green. That book is red.*
can/can't: I can touch the floor. I can't touch the ceiling.
etc.

It is less effective with more conceptually 'remote' structures, such as past **tenses** and **conditionals**, and hence is more appropriate for beginners or younger learners.

Variation 1

Following the 'Total Physical Response' (TPR) method, you give a command and perform the action, while, at the same time, a learner also performs the action:

Walk to the door. Stop. What are we going to do? We're going to open the door. OK. Open the door..., etc.

This is repeated with different learners, the order of the instructions being varied, and new ones added, as learners become increasingly familiar with them.

Strictly speaking, learners simply respond to the commands and do not speak, or at least, not until they feel ready to do so. The idea is that understanding precedes production, often by a long margin. Whatever its merits, TPR is an effective technique for beginners and children. It works well for the teaching of **prepositions**, for example:

Put the pen on the red book. Take the green book and put it next to the red book. Take the pen and put it between the two books ..., etc.

Variation 2

1. Perform a series of actions to the class which they watch. For example, stand up, walk to the window, open it, wave at someone, close the window, turn around, walk back, and sit down.
2. Ask learners, working in pairs, to reconstruct what you did, first speaking, then writing. Check what **tense** they are going to use: the past **tense** is the most suitable, although you could also use this activity to practise *you've just* ... Perform the activities again, if necessary.
3. Ask individuals to read out their sequences, making corrections where necessary; or ask one learner to write the sequence on the board.
4. In pairs, learners repeat the procedure: one performs a series of actions which the other observes. They reverse roles. Then they both write what they saw.

2.17 Situational presentation

Level Any

Time 20–30 minutes

Aims To focus attention on a grammatical item by means of a situation that generates several examples of its use.

Preparation

Plan a situation in advance, choosing one that both generates several examples of the target structure, and which can be set up using vocabulary within the learners' grasp.

Example To teach the future perfect (*will have done*) you could use the following situation:

This is Lynn. She is from Australia. She is going to visit Europe. She only has one month. She has bought a Eurail Pass. She plans to visit all these countries in one month, using her Eurail Pass. What countries is she going to visit ...? What places will she visit in these countries, do you think? What kind of food and drink will she eat? etc.

Procedure

1 Establish the situation using board drawings, and by eliciting details of the context.

2 Having established the situation, focus the learners' attention on those aspects of the situation that determine the choice of grammar item you have selected to highlight. For example:

Does she plan to visit as many countries as possible? (Yes.)
Does she already know her exact route? (No.)
Does she know exactly where she will be at any one time? (No.)
So she doesn't know when she will be in France, for example? (No.)
But what can we say, at least? By the end of the month ...?

At this point some learners may come up with the target structure (either because they are already familiar with it, or because they can deduce it by analogy with their first language and what they already know about English grammar). If they don't come up with it, they should nevertheless by now be optimally positioned in order to make sense of it:

By the end of the month, she *will have been* to France.

3 Highlight the form of the 'model', either by repeating it, by having the learners repeat it, or by writing it on the board—or a

combination of all three. (For complex structures like the future **continuous**, it helps if learners can see as well as hear the model sentence.)

4 Elicit further examples of the target structure, based on the situation, by asking questions or by supplying prompts, for example:

(prompt) *London*
(response) *By the end of the month, she will have been to London.*
(prompt) *Spain*
(response) *By the end of the month, she will have been to Spain.*
(question) *What will she have eaten and drunk in Spain, do you think?*
(response) *She will have eaten paella and drunk sangria.*
etc.

5 Check at regular intervals that learners have understood by asking concept questions:

Does she plan to go to London? (Yes.)
In what time period will she go to London? (This coming month.)
Do we know exactly when she will go to London? (No.)
But, looking back from the end of the month, what can we say? (She will have been to London.)

6 Elicit what Lynn herself predicts about her trip, using the first person:

By the end of the month, I will have been to France, etc.

Practise this, using prompts, in the same way as in Step 4.

7 Write up a representative selection of sentences that have been derived from the situation, in the form of a substitution table:

She	will	have	been	to France
I			climbed	the Eiffel Tower
			seen	the *Mona Lisa.*

8 Ask learners to form true sentences about themselves, beginning *By the end of this week/month/year...*

Variation

Instead of one situation that generates several examples of the target grammar item, it is sometimes easier to devise several, less complicated, situations, each of which generates *one* example of the target item. The following situations, for example, each provide a context for one example of the *will + have done* form:

1 Dan is working overtime this week. He is working about ten hours a day. It is Wednesday evening. So far he has worked 30 hours. By the end of the week ... *he will have worked about 50 hours.*

2 The government wants to build 10,000 new apartments before the end of next year. They have promised that, by the end of next year, the project will be finished. They say that *10,000 new apartments will have been built* by then.

3 Erica is a teacher. It is the end of term. She is marking exams. So far she has marked 50. There are another 50 to mark. She hopes to finish before Sunday evening. By then, *she will have marked 100 exams.*

Comment

Presenting grammar by means of situations gets around the limitations of direct method presentations (see 2.16), and hence has been very popular with teachers who wish to avoid using translation as a way of clarifying the meaning of new structures.

2.18 Dialogue building

Level Any

Time 15–30 minutes

Aims To provide controlled, interactive review of a pre-taught grammar item.

Preparation

Write a short dialogue in which at least one example of the targeted item occurs naturally. The dialogue should not be more than about ten lines in length, and, for the purposes of both memorability and drilling, the lines should not be too long: a maximum of 10–12 syllables each. For example, to practise different past forms (**past simple** and past **continuous**), the following dialogue provides a natural context:

A What happened to you?
B I broke my arm.
A What were you doing?
B I was skiing.
A How did it happen?
B I was going too fast and I fell.
A Does it hurt?
B It did then, but now it's OK.
A You poor thing.

Procedure

1 Set the situation, using drawings of stick figures on the board, for example:

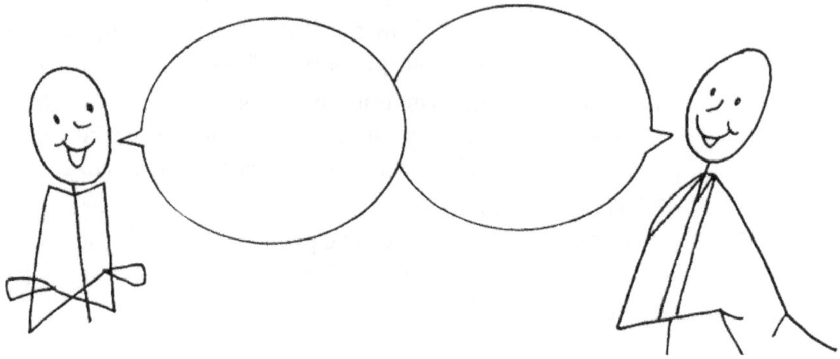

Ask questions to elicit the situation based on visual clues in the picture. For example, *Who are they? Do they know each other? What do you think has happened?* etc.

2 Having established a context and a purpose for the exchange, for example, 'the two people are talking about an accident one of them has had', start to elicit, line by line, the conversation. Elicit the first line (*What happened to you?*) by pointing to the relevant figure on the board and miming surprise. Modify the learners' suggestions in order both to standardize them according to the script you have pre-planned, and to correct any errors (for example, from *What's happened ...?* to *What happened ...?*). At this stage you should not write the lines of the dialogue on the board, but instead encourage learners to memorize them.

3 Drill the first line of the dialogue a few times, both chorally and individually, correcting where necessary, and insisting on natural-sounding rhythm and intonation.

4 Elicit the second line of the dialogue. Again, give some kind of clue, such as pointing to the arm in the sling in the drawing. Drill the line.

5 Now, put the two lines together. (This is why the technique is called 'dialogue *building*'.) Take the role of person A yourself, select a student to take the role of person B, and together perform the first two lines of the dialogue. Do this with one or two more students, then reverse the direction of the exchange, delegating a student to be person A while you take the person B's role.

6 Now, while the rest of the class listen, two students (preferably sitting on opposite sides of the classroom, in order to ensure audibility to all) enact the two-line exchange. This is called *open pairs*. Then two more, and so on. When you think the class is ready, ask them all to practise the exchange with their neighbour (this is called *closed pairs*). Monitor and correct. The complete sequence can be represented like this:

   1 Teacher–student.
   2 Student–teacher.
   3 Student–student (open).
   4 Student–student (closed).

   An alternative to Stage 6 is to divide the class into two halves, and each half choruses its part of the exchange: this works best with young learners.

7 Continue building the dialogue, line by line. Using the interaction model outlined in Stage 6 above, practise the dialogue cumulatively at each stage when there is an even number of lines (i.e. four, six, eight, etc.). It may help students to remember the content and sequence of the exchanges if you provide some kind of word or picture prompt on the board, in descending order, for example:

   happened?... broke ... doing?... skiing ..., etc.

8 When the dialogue has been fully constructed and practised, ask one or two pairs of students to 'perform' it in front of the class.

9 Now, elicit the dialogue back from the students and write it on to the board, so that learners have a copy to take away.

Variation 1

Disappearing dialogue. Write a 6–8 line dialogue on the board and ask learners to read it aloud, and to practise it in pairs. Then, gradually erase words and whole lines from the dialogue. Learners continue practising, each time having to remember more and more of the disappearing dialogue until there is nothing left on the board at all.

Variation 2

Dialogue completion. Write one speaker's half of a dialogue on the board, for example, the overheard part of a telephone conversation. Working together, learners have to reconstruct the original conversation. They then practise and perform it.

Variation 3

Learners' own dialogues. After Stage 1 (setting the situation), ask learners, working in pairs or small groups, to write their own dialogue based on the situation, and including the targeted grammar items (in this case, past simple and past continuous). Monitor this task, providing suggestions and correcting errors. Students then practise their dialogues until they are ready to perform them to the class.

Follow-up

Substitution. Once the original dialogue has been learnt and practised, ask learners to adapt it by changing some of the key information but still retaining the basic outline. For example, in the case of the skiing accident dialogue, ask them to substitute different activities, for example, horse riding, playing football, cycling, etc., and different injuries (a broken leg, a black eye, a sprained ankle, etc.).

Comments

Depending on the level of the class, as well as the predictability of the dialogue, you can either pre-script the dialogue in advance, so that you have a clear idea of the dialogue you want to build, or you can simply construct it as you go along, on the basis of what the learners come up with. A formal situation, such as a shopping encounter, is one which most learners will be familiar with, and therefore should not require a lot of 'scripting' on the part of the teacher. A dialogue between two friends meeting by chance in the street, on the other hand, may require some pre-scripting, since there are so many possible conversational outcomes. Also, to ensure that the targeted grammar item occurs, some pre-scripting is generally advisable.

2.19 Text-based presentation

Level Any

Time 20–30 minutes

Aims To highlight a new grammar item by means of a written text.

Preparation

Choose—or write—a short text that contains two or three instances of the target grammar item(s) used naturally. For example, in order to present the **modal verb** forms *should* and *shouldn't*, the following text could be used:

> Dear Gabby,
>
> I am 13 and I have a sister who is three years older than me. She is always teasing me. She calls me names, like *Fatty*, or *Four-eyes*. What's worse is that she does this in front of my friends. I am really sick of it. What do you think I should do? 'Fed up'
>
> Dear 'Fed up',
>
> It's common for brothers and sisters to tease each other. My advice is that you should just ignore her. It's probably a phase that she's going through. What you shouldn't do is show that you are hurt or embarrassed. This is exactly what she wants. You should remain calm, knowing that it is *her* problem, not yours. But if the problem continues, maybe you should talk to an older person who knows you both.

Make copies of the text for the class.

Procedure

1 Set a general reading task, such as *Who is writing about what? Who to? Why?* in order to establish the context of the text, the kind of text that it is, and its purpose. Learners then read the first letter, and the initial task is checked: in this case, it is a letter to a teen magazine asking for advice about a personal problem. Check that learners understand key vocabulary, such as *tease*.

2 Ask learners to predict what Gabby's response might be. Having discussed this briefly, let them read the response, and compare their ideas with Gabby's. Again, check the meaning of any key vocabulary.

3 Ask learners to identify four pieces of advice that Gabby offers 'Fed-up', and either to underline these or to write them down. These are:

You should just ignore her.
What you shouldn't do is show that you are hurt or embarrassed.
You should remain calm,
Maybe you should talk to an older person.

4 You are now in a position to draw attention to the form and meaning of *should/shouldn't*. You can also highlight the kinds of words and expressions that go with *should*:

you should ***just*** *...*
what *you shouldn't* ***do is*** *...*
maybe *you should ...*

Learners could also be asked to find another example of *should* in the two texts (*What do you think I should do?*).

5 Ask learners to think of other pieces of advice they would give 'Fed up', using *should* and *shouldn't*. They can read these out and discuss the merits of the advice.

Follow-up

Learners can write and exchange 'problem page' letters and then reply to them.

Comments

Because language is always realized as text, any grammar item can be contextualized like this. Certain grammar items (such as **present simple**, **articles**, and **prepositions**) occur in a huge variety of texts. Others have a more restricted range of uses, and it's possible to predict the kind of texts in which they are likely to occur. The **present perfect**, for example, is quite common in news texts; question forms are obviously common in interviews; the **passive** is more common in technical and academic writing; the **modal verbs** *may*, *must*, and *should*, expressing probability, are relatively common in academic writing; the past perfect is relatively common in fiction. Knowing where to look for specific grammar items can help in the selection or design of texts for classroom purposes.

2.20 Input flood

Level Any

Time 15–25 minutes

Aims To raise awareness about a grammar item, by means of repeated exposure of the item.

Preparation

Find or prepare a short text which has a significantly high frequency of a particular grammar item.

Example The following text comes from the Sunday supplement of a British newspaper:

> I like it when I'm listening to my Walkman and the song ends as I arrive at my destination.
>
> I like finding out new words. Here's one for you: crinkum-crankum (*Concise Oxford Dictionary*).
>
> I like seeing a famous sight, buying a postcard and circling the exact location from which I am writing the card.
>
> I like it when the cinema in which I'm seeing a film is actually featured in the film. This occurred when I saw *Breathless* in the Cinema Mac-Mahon in Paris. Everyone laughed.

I like wearing ties worn by my grandfather who died before I was born.
I like any film in which human beings are reduced in size.
I like paying with the exact money.
I like chewing the stopper on the end of a Bic biro.
I like it when people clap at the end of films.
I like red tulips; I like easy-spread butter; I like the first kiss ...

(Abridged from the Patrick Marber column. *The Observer Magazine*, 13 February 1994)

Procedure

1 Distribute the text. Set a general reading task, such as *Who is writing about what? Who to? Why?* in order to establish the context of the text, the kind of text that it is, and its purpose. Check this task.

2 Then, draw attention to the significantly frequent feature. One way of doing this is to ask learners simply to count the number of instances of (in this case) *like*. Then they should categorize these. In this case, the uses of *like* are distributed between *like* + *-ing*, *like* + **noun phrase**, and *like* + *it* + *when*-**clause**.

3 Learners then write their own sentences using the three patterns.

Comments

'Input flood' is the name that some researchers have given to tasks that are designed to cause learners to notice grammar items by virtue of their artificially high frequency in a text. Few authentic texts have a natural 'input flood' of a specific grammar item, but one kind of text that often does is the pop song. Some poetry, too, exploits repetition for its effects.

Example The following poem repeats the structure *verb* + *object* + *(object) complement*:

Call alligator long-mouth
call alligator saw-mouth
call alligator pushy-mouth
call alligator scissors mouth
call alligator raggedy mouth
call alligator bumpy-bum
call alligator all dem rude word
but better wait
till you cross river.

(John Agard. 'Don't call alligator long-mouth till you cross river' from *Say It Again Granny*. Bodley Head, 1986. Reprinted in *Poems on the Underground* (tenth edition) Cassell, 2001)

ELT coursebooks used to include texts based on the principle of 'input flood', but this practice has gone out of fashion, on the grounds that such texts lacked authenticity. But authenticity is not 'sacred', and it may need to be sacrificed in the interests of clarity.

Example Here is a text from a coursebook published in 1978:

> Look at this man.
> His name's Terry Archer.
> He isn't from London.
> He's from Oxford.
> He's a factory worker.
> He's got a good job.
> He's got a car.
> He hasn't got a big house, he's got a flat.
> He's got a wife, but he hasn't got any children.
> Life's all right.
>
> (B. Hartley and P. Viney. *Streamline English Departures*, Unit 16. Oxford University Press, 1978)

Short of finding naturally occurring examples of such texts, teachers may need to write their own.

2.21 Dictogloss

Level Any

Time 15–30 minutes

Aims To raise learners' awareness about differences between their evolving mental grammar and the target language grammar; to learn from each other doing a collaborative task.

Preparation

Find or write a short text—it shouldn't be longer than 100 words, and it should be complete. Insert a number of instances of the target grammar item. For example, here is a short (80-word) text, taken from a book of children's jokes:

> Three men were stuck on a desert island and a fairy came along and offered them a free wish each. 'I wish I was back with my family and friends,' said the first man, and in a flash he disappeared back home. 'I too wish I was back with my family and friends,' said the next man, and he too disappeared. 'It's very lonely here,' said the last man. 'I wish my two friends were here with me ...!'
>
> (Brough Girling. *The Great Puffin Joke Directory*. Puffin Books, 1990)

This text is good because it follows a recognizable three-part joke structure, and therefore is easier to process than a text whose organization is less readily identifiable. What's more, it includes some repetition. It also includes a grammar item that learners at intermediate level might not produce automatically, that is *wish* plus past tense: *I wish I was back ... I wish my two friends were here ...*

Procedure

1 Read a short text to the class while they simply listen.

2 As soon as you have finished, tell the class to write down any words, expressions, even sentences they can still remember.

3 Allow learners to compare notes in pairs, and to write a joint version of the text.

4 Read the text again, and then allow time for learners, in their pairs, to make any amendments.

5 If seating allows, put the pairs together in groups of four so that they can compare notes, and produce a new, collaborative, version of the text. Read the text aloud again, if the learners feel the need for it.

6 You can then ask one of the learners to come forward to the board, and act as the 'class secretary', transcribing on to the board a definitive version of the text based on the combined suggestions of all the class. At this stage, you should not intervene until this latest version of the text is completely transcribed.

7 Read the text aloud again, pausing after each sentence, to allow learners to confirm or not the accuracy of the text on the board, and to make any necessary changes. (Alternatively, you can project the original text on to the board, alongside the class's version, using an overhead projector.) Once the class's text has been amended, it is now 'available' for a focus on the language embedded in it. First, though, you should check that the meaning of the text is clear, by asking questions about the story (for example, *Where does it take place? Who are the people in it?*) and by checking any unfamiliar vocabulary (for example, *in a flash*).

8 Ask learners to identify, and comment on, the differences between their own texts and the original text. Some of these differences may simply be due to different but correct ways of saying the same thing. Other differences may have resulted in errors. Make sure that learners correct these. Some of the errors are likely to be in the form of the targeted structure. It is possible, for example, that the learners may have captured the sense—but not the exact words—of the 'wishes' in the text. For example, instead of *I wish I was back* they may have written *I wish I am back or I wish to be back*. This difference offers an opportunity to highlight both the form and the meaning of the hypothetical *wish* construction.

Alternatively, ask learners simply to underline all examples of *wish* in their own texts, and, once these are identified, to generalize a rule about the grammar of *wish*, i.e. that you use the past tense for present wishes.

Variation

During stage 2 above, record yourself saying the text. This allows you to replay the text so that learners can hear it in exactly the same way they first heard it. More importantly, it allows you to improvise the text, rather than read it from a script, which, because it sounds more natural, is usually also more intelligible.

Follow-up

Learners can write their own texts, using your text as a model, and incorporating the targeted language features that you have highlighted.

Comments

Any item of grammar that can be embedded in a short text is suitable for this kind of treatment. It's a good idea to ensure that the grammar items that are chosen are slightly beyond your estimate of the class's competence, but that the surrounding text is within their competence. This way they will be able to make sense of the items, even though they may not be able to reproduce them exactly. They will therefore be in a good position to 'notice' these items. A lot of the value of this exercise also comes from the discussions they have in comparing their versions of the text and in negotiating a consensus version. These discussions should not be cut short too soon, therefore, and, especially at lower levels, can be allowed to take place in the learners' first language.

Acknowledgements

For more ideas on how to use this technique (also called *dictocomp* and *grammar dictation*), and for more example texts, see *Grammar Dictation*, by Ruth Wajnryb, in this series.

2.22 Emergent grammar

Level Intermediate and above

Time 25–40 minutes

Aims To focus on those grammar items that 'emerge' from a speaking task.

Procedure

1 Set up a short activity that involves learners speaking in 'open class', i.e. while the rest of the class is listening. For example, ask learners to write, individually, on a slip of paper the name of one memorable thing that they have eaten or drunk in the last 24 hours.

2 Collect in the slips of paper. Take one at random (which might say *chocolate cake*, for example). Get the 'author' of that slip to elaborate by asking him or her questions, such as *Where did you have the cake? Who made it? What did you have with it? Do you often eat chocolate cake?* etc.

3 Then take out another slip and repeat the process, and so on until you have 'interviewed' five to eight learners.

4 While the learners are answering your questions, note down any 'useful' language that comes up. In this case, it might be sentences in the past tense, or it might be the use of verbs like *taste*, *smell*, etc. + adjective, or expressions using the passive, like *it was made of …*, *it was served with …*, etc. These sentences might be the corrected versions of what the learners have actually said. Write these down on a piece of paper, or directly on to an overhead transparency, while trying not to slow the pace of the interaction too much. Six to eight sentences will be sufficient for the subsequent grammar focus.

5 Once the question-and-answer stage is over, write up the sentences you have collected on to the board (or project them), and use them as the 'data' for a grammar focus. If, for example, all the sentences have a grammar feature in common (such as the past tense, or the passive), ask the learners to identify it, and to explain the rules of formation and use.

Follow-up

Working in pairs or small groups, learners recall and reconstruct the 'stories' that you have elicited in Stage 2. To help them do this, write up the names of the items of food and drink that were discussed (for example, *chocolate cake*). They write a short summary of each of the interactions, incorporating the targeted grammar features where appropriate.

Example Iannis had a piece of chocolate cake this morning with his coffee. He bought it in the café opposite his flat. It was freshly baked, and it tasted delicious. He can't remember exactly how much it cost, but it was worth it.

Comments

Using learners' output as data for a grammar focus is a fairly high-risk strategy, in that it is impossible to predict—and therefore, to fully control—what the learners will say. Nevertheless, certain topics tend to give rise to certain grammar structures, and the clever placement of questions can often help direct the interaction towards the grammar item you have pre-selected. For example, to elicit *going to* to talk about plans, ask learners to write down on their slips of paper one thing that they are looking forward to doing in the next 24 hours. Or to elicit *would* to talk about imaginary situations, ask them to write down the name of a famous person they would like to invite to dinner.

Acknowledgements

Thanks to Luke Meddings for this idea.

2.23 Using realia

Level Any

Time 20–30 minutes

Aims To introduce a grammar item by means of real objects (*realia*).

Materials A collection of real objects, depending on the grammar area you are planning to focus on. For example, the contents of a 'mystery person's' handbag can be used to create sentences in the present simple (*She takes the bus; she shops at X supermarket ...*). Or a variety of personal items gathered from the learners, such as keys, mobile phones, wrist watches, etc., can be used to teach *Whose is this?/Whose are these?* and *It's Dani's. They're hers. It's mine.* etc.

Procedure

1 Assemble the real objects and check that learners know what each one is called. If the class size allows, the objects can be passed around.

2 Use the objects to elicit sentences, for example:

TEACHER (*holding up pen*) Whose is this pen?
STUDENT 1 Vuong.
TEACHER Listen. *It's Vuong's. It's Vuong's.* Whose is it?
STUDENT 1 It's Vuong's.
TEACHER Vuong, is this your pen?
STUDENT 2 Yes.
TEACHER Listen: *Yes, it's mine.* Vuong, is this your pen?
STUDENT 2 Yes, it's mine.
etc.

3 Write the sentences that you have elicited on to the board, and draw attention to their grammatical form.

Variation

Use family photographs as realia to teach **possessive determiners** (*That's my father...*) and possessive *'s: That's Lin's brother*. They are also useful for practising **prepositions** and present tense verb forms: *Lin is standing next to her son. The person sitting on the sofa is my sister*, as well as the verb forms that incorporate these items: *Who is the person holding the baby?*

Ask learners, in advance, to bring their family photographs to class. They can be asked to prepare a short description of their photos beforehand, and to ask and answer questions about each other's photos in pairs or small groups.

2.24 Output flood

Level Any

Time 25–30 minutes

Aims To encourage frequent production of a targeted grammar item in a creative context.

Preparation

Choose a grammar item. Design a 'rubric'—or sentence starters—which will encourage the learners to produce the grammar item several times.

Example A rubric designed to elicit at least eight instances of the **present perfect** might be:

I've never _____
I've never _____
I've never _____
I've never _____
But I've always wanted to.

I've never ________
I've never _____
I've never _____
I've never _____
And I've never wanted to.

Write a completed version which is about yourself, for example,

I've never been to Kathmandu.
I've never seen a comet.
etc.

I've never seen a ghost.
I've never been chased by a lion ...
etc.

Procedure

1 Write the rubric on the board, or project it by means of an overhead or data projector. Tell the learners to listen as you read your own version of the text.

2 In pairs, the learners then try to reconstruct from memory what went in each space.

3 Allow time for some discussion of your own text. Encourage questions, such as *Why have you always wanted to go to Kathmandu? Why have you never wanted to see a ghost?*

4 Individually, learners write their own texts, using the rubric as a model.

5 In pairs or small groups, they exchange texts, and ask each other questions about the texts, as in Stage 3 above.

Follow-up

The texts could be displayed as poems. See *Creative Poetry Writing* in this series.

Acknowledgements

The idea for this activity comes from *Creative Grammar Practice*, Gerngross, G. & Puchta, H. Pilgrims Longman, 1992.

2.25 Information gap—spot the difference

Level Any

Time 10–20 minutes

Aims To provide interactive conditions for reinforcing a grammar item.

Materials Sufficient copies of the two versions of the same picture to be distributed to pairs.

Procedure

1 Distribute the pictures so that each member of a pair has a different version of the same picture. They should hold the pictures and be seated in such a way that they cannot see each other's picture.

2 Point out that the pictures are different in a number of details, and demonstrate the kind of exchange necessary in order to discover the differences. For lower levels it will help to write some question 'frames' on the board, such as:

Is there a man/woman, etc. standing/sitting next to/behind/in front of ...?
What is he/she doing?
Has he/she got ...?

3 Learners take turns to ask each other questions until they have discovered all the differences.

4 They then write up the differences, using a rubric such as:

In picture A there is ..., but in picture B ...

Comments

While this activity can result in a lot of interaction, it is relatively limited in terms of the structures that can be practised. These comprise mostly those structures used for describing ongoing activities, such as the present continuous, *there is/are ...; has/have got;* and **prepositions**.

Variation

Describe and draw. In this variation, only one of each pair has a picture. Those with the pictures describe it to their partners, who have to try and reproduce the picture. This works well for practice of **prepositions**, for example.

2.26 Jigsaw mingling

Level Any

Time 10–15 minutes

Aims To review a grammar item in an interactive way.

Procedure

1 In this example, *going to* is practised. Start by drawing a grid on the board, like this:

2 Elicit three holiday destinations known to your students. Write these in the first column.

3 Then elicit three months when people often go on holiday, for example, March, August, December. Write these in the second column.

4 Next, elicit three hotel names, such as *The Grand, The Ritz, The Holiday Inn*, and write these in the third column.

5 Finally, elicit three holiday activities, such as deep-sea diving, sunbathing, and windsurfing.

6 Tell the class they are to plan a holiday, and that they should each (secretly) choose one destination, one month, one hotel, and one activity.

7 Check the questions that they will need to find out the holiday plans of the other learners by asking questions such as:

Where are you going to go?
When are you going to go?
Where are you going to stay?
What are you going to do?

8 The learners now have to stand up, walk around and ask as many other learners as possible about their holiday plans, noting the names of any other learners who have chosen the same 'package' as they have.

9 At the end of the activity they can report back, in order to find out what was the most popular package. (If there is not room to stand up and mingle, learners can form groups with adjacent learners, in order to ask their questions.)

Comments

You can adjust the grid to suit the size of the group, adding or taking away rows and columns, so that there are more or fewer combinations, as desired. Columns to add might be length of visit and mode of travel. This task can be adapted to other language areas, such as the **past simple**—using the same prompts but this time the holiday was in the past. Or the **present simple**, as in a 'blind date' situation: *What kind of music do you like? What's your star sign? What sport do you play?*

2.27 Surveys and questionnaires

Level Elementary and above

Time 20–30 minutes

Aims To provide practice of grammar items in communicative interaction.

Procedure

1 Set a theme and an objective for a survey/questionnaire. For example, the theme might be *freedoms*, and the object of the survey is to find out who had the strictest—and who had the least strict—upbringing. Elicit some example questions, directing attention to the grammar structures that should be incorporated. For example:

Did your parents let you choose your own clothes?
At school, did they make you cut your hair?
Were you allowed to stay out late, if you wanted to?

2 In small groups, learners design more questions. Each member of the group should write the questions on to a piece of paper.

3 Regroup the learners so that new groups are formed consisting of one learner each from all of the original groups. (One way of doing this is to assign each student in each group a number, say, 1, 2, and 3. Then ask all the number 1s to sit together, all the number 2s to sit together, etc.)

4 The learners take turns to ask each other their questions, noting the replies.

5 They then return to their original groups, to report and collate the results of their survey. They should be prepared to report to the class some of their more interesting findings, using a rubric such as this one:

All/Most/Some of the class were allowed to ...
The person with the strictest/least strict upbringing was ...
This is because his/her parents made him/her ... didn't let him/her ...
etc.

Follow-up

Learners can now write up their survey findings, taking care to include the targeted grammar items.

Comments

The survey format can be adapted to virtually any topic and grammar item, for example:

Whose daily routine is the most unusual? *When do you …*
Who is a creature of habit? *How often do you …?*
How adventurous are you? *Would you ever…?*
Who has strange tastes? *Have you ever eaten/drunk …?*
Whose weekend was the most boring? *Did you …/What did you …?*
Who is the most skilful? *Can you …? Do you know how to …?*

2.28 Guessing games

Level Any

Time 5–20 minutes

Aims To encourage the frequent use of specific grammar items in a game-type activity.

Preparation

Choose the theme of the game according to what grammar item you wish to practise. For example, to elicit questions with *can* and *have got*, guessing an animal works well. For practising the past tense, choose famous non-living people as the theme. For practising **present simple** and *have to*, the variety of the game called 'What's my line?' where jobs have to be guessed, is effective.

Procedure

1 Demonstrate the game by telling learners that they have to find out what animal, person, job, etc., you are thinking about, by asking **yes/no questions**. Elicit some sample questions and write the patterns for these on the board.

Examples For an animal guessing game:

Can you fly/swim/climb trees/run fast, etc.?
Have you got four legs/wings/a tail/horns, etc.?

For 'What's my line?':

Do you work outdoors/work with children, etc.?
Do you have to train a long time/wear a uniform, etc.?

For a famous non-living person:

Were you famous for…?
Did you invent/discover/write/paint/compose something?

2 Once learners have guessed who or what you are, they then take turns to think of mystery items themselves, and to be asked questions. This can either take the form of one learner in front of the class being asked questions by the rest of the class (suitable for small classes) or students working in groups of various sizes, or in pairs.

2.29 Alibis

Level Intermediate and above

Time 20–30 minutes

Aims To review past tense verb forms.

Procedure

1 Two students are 'accused' of having committed some crime, such as a robbery in the institution where the class takes place, in a fixed period, say, between the hours of 10 and 11 in the morning on the preceding day. The two 'accused' then have to establish an alibi, and they go out of the room to do this. The alibi needs to account for their actions only during the time period in question (anything before or after is irrelevant), and it is important to establish that they were together for all that time.

2 While the accused are working out their alibi, the rest of the class (with the teacher prompting, if necessary) can prepare generic questions of the type: *What were you doing ...? What did you do next? Did you meet anyone? What did you say? How much did it cost? Who paid?* etc. The accused are then led in, one at a time, and have to answer the questions put to them. (It helps to establish the rule that they are not allowed to say 'I don't remember'.) Any significant discrepancy in their answers means that they are, of course, guilty.

With large classes, Alibis can be played in groups, each group playing their own version of the game. Alternatively, (and so long as they are out of earshot) the two accused can be interviewed simultaneously by two different groups, and then exchange places.

Variation 1

Green Card. 'Immigration officers' interview, separately, two candidates who claim to be members of the same family (in which case, they have to answer questions about the other members of their immediate family—their names, age, and appearance), or who claim to be partners (in which case, they have to answer questions about their daily routine). This is good for practising present tense forms and the language of description.

Variation 2

UFO. Two people are interviewed separately by *The Institute of Paranormal Research* about an encounter with aliens that they claim to have experienced. They are questioned separately about the exact details of the encounter, in order to check that it is authentic. This is good for practising past tense forms and the language of description.

2.30 Problem-solving presentation (using pictures)

Level Pre-intermediate and above

Time 20–30 minutes

Aims To draw learners' attention, using pictures, to a conceptual distinction that they may not have previously noticed, or which they may not have thought significant.

Preparation

1 Prepare a set of pictures that illustrate a distinction between two contrasting grammar items. The pictures can either be photocopied for distribution to learners, or displayed in the form of an overhead transparency.

Example To focus on the difference between *to do something* and *to have something done* you could use the following pictures:

Jackie

Pam

Jim

Lucy

Helen

John

Mike

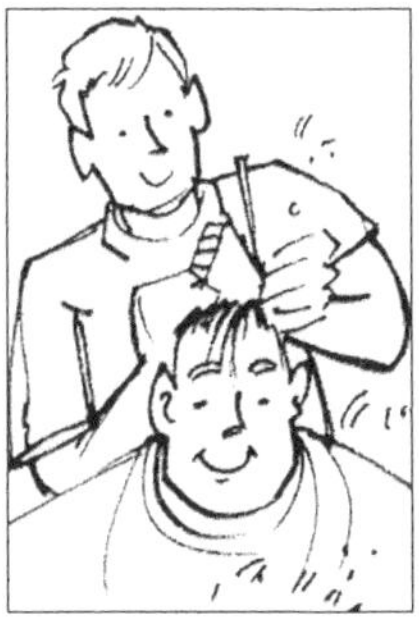

Joe

2 Prepare questions that incorporate these grammar items, for example:

Who painted her house herself?
Who had her house painted?
Who cut his own hair?
Who had his hair cut?
Who had her photo taken?
Who took a photo of herself?
Who had his shirts ironed?
Who ironed his own shirts?

Procedure

1 Draw attention to the pictures. Ask the prepared questions, repeating when necessary.

2 Provide clear feedback on the answers to each question, for example:

TEACHER Who had her photo taken?
STUDENT 1 Lucy.
TEACHER No. Listen again: who had her photo taken?
STUDENT 1 Helen.
TEACHER Yes. Helen had her photo taken.

3 If learners remain confused after the first three or four questions, write the questions on the board. This will help focus their attention on the difference in form between, for example:

Who painted her house?
Who had her house painted?

4 If learners are still uncertain as to the difference, write the answers to the questions:

Jackie painted her house.
Pam had her house painted.

Try and elicit—by reference to the pictures—the difference in meaning. Then continue asking the questions about the other pictures.

5 If you have written the sentences on the board, rub them off. Then ask learners in pairs to write sentences for each of the pictures, using the targeted grammar forms.

Comments

The rationale behind this kind of activity is to 'problematize' a grammar distinction that learners may not have noticed or thought significant. By stripping the situation down to the difference between sentence pairs, learners are forced to attend to the grammar distinction, at the level, initially, of understanding rather than production. For this reason, such activities are sometimes called *grammar interpretation* tasks. Other grammar distinctions that lend themselves to this approach include:

- **active** vs **passive** (*The boy was chased by a dog* vs *The boy chased a dog*);
- **verbs** that can be both **transitive** and **intransitive**: *The ship sank* vs *The ship was sunk*);

- **present perfect** vs **past simple** (*She has been waiting for three hours* vs *She waited for three hours*);
- **past simple** vs **past continuous** (*The plane was landing* vs *The plane landed*);
- **countable** vs **uncountable nouns**: (*He is carrying a paper* vs *He is carrying paper*).

2.31 Problem-solving presentation (using text)

Level Pre-intermediate and above

Time 20–30 minutes

Aims To draw learners' attention, using a text, to a conceptual distinction that they may not have previously noticed, or which they may not have thought significant.

Preparation

Write a text and associated comprehension questions in such a way that the questions require learners to discriminate between two contrasting grammar items. The items can either be in the text itself, or in the questions about the text. For example, see Worksheet 2.31a, designed to alert learners to the way *used to* is used to refer to past habits, and habitual states, and how it contrasts with the **present simple** for present habits and habitual states. Make a copy of the prepared text for each learner.

Procedure

1 Distribute the text and allow learners time to read it silently. Check the meaning of any vocabulary likely to be unfamiliar.

2 Ask Questions 1 and 2. Depending on their familiarity with the form *used to*, learners may not appreciate that it differs from the **present simple**, and answer either *Jenny* or *Jamie* indiscriminately. Give clear feedback on their answers. For example:

TEACHER Who used to live in Italy?
STUDENT 1 Jamie.
TEACHER No. Listen: who *used* to live in Italy? etc.

3 Work through a few more questions in open class, just to make sure that the learners have got the general idea, and then let them work individually or in pairs on the rest.

4 Check the answers and elicit a rule about the use of *used to*, i.e. that it is used only to talk about *past* habits or habitual states.

5 Learners can then rewrite the texts, substituting *used to* where appropriate.

6 Finally, they can write short texts about themselves, incorporating *used to*.

Worksheet 2.31a
Jenny and Jamie

Jenny lived in Italy for two years and then she moved to France. She worked as an English teacher in Italy, and she does the same in France. She was married to an Italian, but now she is divorced. She plays tennis a lot, and she writes poetry.

Jamie has lived in Italy for five years now. Before that he lived in France. He worked as an English teacher in France. Now he's a writer. He wrote poetry when he was young but now he writes travel books. His wife is a cook. In his free time Jamie goes sailing. He played tennis in his youth, but now he says he's too fat.

1 *Who used to live in Italy?*
2 *Who lives in Italy?*
3 *Who used to live in France?*
4 *Who lives in France?*
5 *Who used to be an English teacher?*
6 *Who is an English teacher?*
7 *Who is married?*
8 *Who used to be married?*
9 *Who plays tennis?*
10 *Who used to play tennis?*
11 *Who writes poetry?*
12 *Who used to write poetry?*

Variation

Worksheet 2.31b is an example of a task in which the targeted grammar items are *included* in the text, rather than in the questions that follow it. The task hinges on learners understanding the difference between the **past simple**, to talk about a time period that is 'detached' from the present (because the person referred to is dead), and the **present perfect**, to talk about a time period that still has present relevance (because the person referred to is alive).

Worksheet 2.31b

Here are two texts that have been mixed up. One is about Arthur Miller and the other is about David Mamet. Can you sort them out?

Arthur Miller was born in New York in 1915, and died in 2005.
David Mamet was born in Illinois in 1947.
He lived most of his life in New York.
He has lived mostly in New York.
He has worked as an actor, director, and writer.
He worked as a writer and director, but never acted.
He wrote many plays and screenplays.
He has written many plays and screenplays.
He also wrote two travel books.
He has also taught drama.
He has been married twice, and has three children.
He was married twice—once to the film star Marilyn Monroe.

The two texts are:

Arthur Miller was born in New York in 1915, and died in 2005. He lived most of his life in New York. He worked as a writer and director, but never acted. He wrote many plays and screenplays. He also wrote two travel books. He was married twice—once to the film star Marilyn Monroe.

David Mamet was born in Illinois in 1947. He has lived mostly in New York. He has worked as an actor, director, and writer. He has written many plays and screenplays. He has also taught drama. He has been married twice, and has three children.

Comments

As with Activity 2.30, the above tasks, by creating a grammar 'problem', are designed to raise awareness about conceptual distinctions that might otherwise go unnoticed.

2.32 'Grammaring' sentences

Level Intermediate and above

Time 25–40 minutes

Aims To develop learners' understanding of how grammar helps fine-tune the meanings expressed in words only.

Preparation

Write one or more 'degrammarized' sentences, that is, sentences that have been reduced to **content words** only, like a telegram or a newspaper headline, for example:

BICYCLE STEAL WOMAN
PRESIDENT WELCOME KING
GIVE PRIZE WRITER CHARITY

Procedure

1 Write the degrammarized sentence (or sentences) on the board.

2 Put learners into pairs or small groups. Ask them to create as many sentences as they can from these words. Tell them that they can change the order and form of the words, and you can add **articles**, **prepositions**, relative **pronouns**, and **auxiliary verbs**. You can set a time limit and the pair or group to come up with the most *plausible* sentences, is the winner.

Example Possible combinations of the elements BICYCLE STEAL WOMAN include:

The woman's bicycle was stolen.
A woman's bicycle has been stolen.
A woman stole a bicycle.
Women are stealing bicycles.
A woman's bicycle is being stolen.
Women's bicycles will be stolen
Woman: steal the bicycle!
It was a woman who stole the bicycle.
What was stolen was the woman's bicycle.
The bicycle that would've been stolen was the woman's.
etc.

Follow-up

Challenge learners to think of natural-sounding contexts for the sentences they have created.

2.33 'Grammaring' a text

Level Intermediate and above

Time 25–40 minutes

Aims To develop learners' understanding of how grammar helps fine-tune the meanings expressed in words only.

Materials

Copies of 'degrammarized' text.

Preparation

Prepare a 'degrammarized' text, that is, a text that has been stripped of its grammatical features and consists just of **content words**.

Example ONE DAY FRIEND SUGGEST GO FISH BOAT GET UP EARLY SET OUT BEFORE DAWN BEAUTIFUL DAY SUN SHINE SEA CALM HAVE WONDERFUL TIME CATCH MANY FISH SUDDENLY COME BACK SHORE WIND BEGIN BLOW SEA BECOME ROUGH BOAT MOTOR STOP WORK RADIO HELP COASTGUARD COME MANAGE RESCUE RETURN SAFELY LAND NEVER GO FISH LITTLE BOAT AGAIN!

Procedure

1 Distribute the text. Check that learners are familiar with the meaning of all the words.

2 They then work individually, in pairs, or small groups to 'add the grammar' and create a fully degrammarized text. Point out, though, that there is not one 'correct' answer. Rather, there are many different possibilities, depending on the kind of meanings and nuances that the writer wants to express. As an example, contrast *a friend*, *my friend*, and *a friend of mine*—all well formed degrammarizations of FRIEND, but each conveys a slightly different kind of relation. *A friend* means one of several friends, but not one in particular; *my friend* suggests a particular friend, possibly a close friend; whereas *a friend of mine* emphasizes the relationship to me without suggesting that the friend is special.

3 Monitor the writing stage, providing feedback where necessary, and indicating where the grammarization process has resulted in either ill-formed sentences or incoherent text.

4 Ask learners to exchange, read, and comment on, each other's texts.

5 Provide an example version of the text of your own, either as a handout or projected on to the board. Again, point out that this is only one version of the text. Invite questions, using the rubric: *Instead of X, could you say Y?*

Example Here is a 'grammarized' version of the above text:

> One day a friend of mine suggested we go fishing in his boat. We got up early and set out before dawn. It was a beautiful day. The sun was shining and the sea was calm. We were having a wonderful time and we caught many fish. Suddenly, as we were coming back to shore the wind began to blow and the sea became rough. Then the boat's motor stopped working and we had to radio for help. The coastguard came and managed to rescue us and we returned safely to land. But I'll never go fishing in a little boat again!

Variation 1

Hand out a short text (about fifty words maximum) and ask learners to 'degrammarize' it—that is, strip it of its grammar attributes and turn it into simply words (like a telegram). They should write the words on to a piece of paper. Remove or hide the original text, and let the learners attempt to reconstruct it from memory, putting the grammar back.

Variation 2

Different groups have different texts, which they strip down, and then exchange. They then try and reconstruct the texts, before comparing their versions with the original.

2.34 Grammar mastermind

Level Intermediate and above

Time 20–30 minutes

Aims To revise an area—or areas—of grammar, and to test one another.

Materials A grammar reference or guide, for example, of the type found in most coursebooks, or a student grammar with or without exercises.

Procedure

1 Explain the objective of the task, i.e. to prepare a grammar quiz to test other groups. Identify the grammar topics to be tested—they may be topics recently covered, or topics that are scheduled for a forthcoming review (in which case the quiz will serve as a kind of 'agenda organizer'). All groups can work on the same area, or different grammar areas can be allocated to different groups.

2 Distribute student grammars, or refer learners to the relevant sections of their coursebooks. Learners work in groups to prepare questions about the designated topics. You can give examples of different question rubrics:

Examples

How do you form ...?
When do you use ...?
What's the past/infinitive/negative/question form, etc. of ...?
What's the difference (in meaning) between ...?
Is this sentence correct?

Monitor the learners at work, checking that their answers are correct and make sure the groups keep a separate record of the answers to their questions.

3 Groups exchange quizzes, and answer them, without reference to their grammars.

4 They then send them back for 'marking', and these are returned once more, with marks, comments, and explanations, where appropriate.

Variation 1

A class of around 8–10 students can be divided into two groups. Having prepared their questions, each group takes a turn as the quiz contestants, to whom the other group ask their questions orally, in open class. The teacher keeps a record of the points won by each team. Alternatively, a representative of each group can be chosen to answer the questions put to him or her by the other group.

Variation 2

The class can work in groups to prepare questions to ask the *teacher* about a specific area of grammar. This could be done, less in the spirit of testing the teacher, than in finding out answers to the questions that the learners themselves want answered, in the spirit of a kind of 'grammar clinic'. In other words, an ask-the-teacher session could take the place of a traditional grammar presentation.

Follow-up

Learners, working in pairs or small groups, can design exercises to test knowledge of the grammar areas that were the focus of the quiz, and which are then exchanged for completion. For ideas for different exercise types—such as gap-fill exercises, sentence transformations, and sentence completions—direct their attention to examples in their coursebooks and workbooks.

2.35 Internet hunt

Level Intermediate to advanced

Time 20–50 minutes

Aims To practise using the Internet as a tool to explore grammar and find authentic examples.

Materials None, but Internet access—either in school or at home—is essential.

Procedure

1 Ask students to brainstorm commonly co-occurring strings of words—or **chunks**—that are typically associated with a particular structure. For example, if the target structure is second **conditional** sentences, typical strings might be *wouldn't it be great if*, *what would you do if*, and *I would if I could*. Typical third conditional strings might be *if only I hadn't*, *if I'd known that*, or *would never have*.

2 Ask students to search for instances of these chunks on the Internet, using a search engine such as Google (see Further Reading, p.128). They should not only find examples of the chunk but note the context in which the chunk occurs, such as the kind of text, as well as any co-occurring structures or **lexical phrases**. Often the 'search results' page will provide the item in a sentence-length context, but it will be necessary to go to the web page where the item occurs in order to find its text-length context.

Example A search for *wouldn't it be great if* instantly produced these eight examples:

1 **Wouldn't it be great if** we could find an energy source that was actually better than oil? It would be incredibly terrific if that new energy source was so abundant that we could not even begin to calculate how long it would last.
2 **Wouldn't It Be Great If** We All Spoke the Same Language?
3 **Wouldn't it be great if** your nearsightedness could be corrected while you sleep? It might sound far-fetched, but it's a reality for some people and is available throughout the country.
4 **Wouldn't It Be Great If** France Rejected the EU Constitution?
5 **Wouldn't it be great if** you could help a sick child in under one minute without spending any money? I've never before sent an

'everyone in my address book' email, but this time I am doing it, because, I have a way you can.

6 **Wouldn't It Be Great If** Angels Had Wings?

7 Even though you don't want to stop going to your acupuncturist, **wouldn't it be great if** you could also do it for yourself?

8 **Wouldn't it be great if** we could look forward to a whole world in which no child will be left behind?

3 Ask learners to identify any grammar patterns or rules associated with the chunk. In this case, it is the use of the past tense form in the *if*-**clause**: *spoke, rejected, had, could.*

4 Ask learners to draw up a 'profile' of the chunk, to include such information as

- typical text type;
- position in text;
- associated structures;
- associated words/chunks.

Example A profile of *wouldn't it be great if* produces the following facts:

- typical text type: advertising or persuasive texts (examples 1–7);
- position in text: often the title (for example, examples 2, 4, and 6) or the first line (examples 1, 3, and 5);
- associated structures: **modal verbs**: *would, could, might*;
- associated words/chunks: positive words like *incredibly terrific, corrected, help, look forward to.*

5 Learners can then write their own text beginning or including *Wouldn't it be great if …*, incorporating features they have noted in the profile.

Comments

The search for grammar items need not involve searching the entire Internet, but can be restricted to a specific website or even a specific text, if it is long enough. Most newspaper websites have a search facility, which allows you to search the current edition or archived back numbers. For example, using the *Independent* website (see Further Reading, p.128), and searching in the editions of just one week, the following six examples of the pattern *going to go* were found:

1 the movement is **going to go** into decline
2 if I ever get the chance, I'm **going to go** there.
3 We thought we were **going to go** home, but then he was released.
4 players who were **going to go** on and average 40 or 50 for England.
5 It was not **going to go** any faster.
6 This is part of an ongoing theme, and it's not **going to go** away

All but one example (5) occurred in quoted speech, suggesting that this string is more typical of spoken than of written grammar.

A search of just one text—a twenty-chapter novel chosen at random from the Project Gutenberg website (see Further Reading, p.128)—produced only one example of *going to go*:

> Do you remember that place you found, in Maine, I think? You babbled about it. Said you were **going to go** there if ever you wanted to get out of the world.
>
> (Marie Conway Oemloer. *The Purple Heights*)

(Searching for words or **phrases** on a web page is easy using the instruction 'Search on this page' in the 'Edit' menu.) This single instance of *going to go* in the novel compares with a total of sixty-seven occurrences of *going to* with other **verbs**, including fifteen occurrences of *going to be* and six of *going to do*. A closer examination of these examples would reveal how many occur in quoted speech compared with how many occur in the body of the text itself.

Comments

For more ideas about using the Internet to research grammar questions, see *The Internet* by S. Windeatt, D. Hardisty, and D. Eastment, in this series.

3
Text grammar

Introduction

Look at this sentence: *The dog had eaten it.* This is a grammatically well formed sentence, but it makes little sense since a number of its grammatical features can be interpreted only by reference to a larger context, including whatever text preceded the sentence in question. The use of the definite **article** *the*, for example, suggests that the writer believes that the dog is known to the reader, perhaps because of some previous mention in the text, or perhaps because reader and writer share a world that includes a known dog. The use of the past perfect (*had eaten*) situates the event prior to another event which, again, we can only assume has already been mentioned in the 'missing' text. Likewise, the thing referred to by *it* is not recoverable without recourse to the preceding text, which may have been something like: *I couldn't hand my homework in. (The dog had eaten it.)*

This small example serves to show how grammar extends 'beyond the sentence'. That is to say, a lot of grammar is intelligible only in context. If it is intelligible only in context, it is probably best studied and practised only in context, too. However, for reasons of convenience and economy, a great deal of traditional grammar teaching has been limited to the study of grammar as realized in single, decontextualized, sentences—despite the fact that most language in use occurs, not as sentences, but as cohesive *text*.

What, though, constitutes a *context?* We have seen that, in the case of *the dog*, the context might include the world in which reader and writer (or speaker and listener) cohabit, as when one person says to another *Have you fed the dog?* This kind of context is a real-world, extra-linguistic, one. On the other hand, in this text extract: *I was kept awake half the night by the barking of a dog. Apparently, the dog belonged to the landlord ...* the dog in the second sentence is identifiable, not by reference to a real-world context, but by reference to the preceding text, i.e. the first sentence. This is the *linguistic* context. For convenience, we will call the former (real-world) context a sentence's *context*, and the latter, linguistic one, a sentence's *co-text*.

The activities in Part 3 look at the way that grammar choices are determined by, and are often only intelligible in the light of, these contextual and co-textual environments. For convenience we will call this perspective on grammar *text grammar*, since it is largely through the study of texts that its functions and characteristics are properly understood. However, it would be equally correct to call it *context grammar*, since it attempts to explain grammar by reference to its typical contexts (and co-texts) of use. It has also been called *discourse grammar*, discourse being a more general term than *text*, and implying a concern for spoken texts as well as written ones.

3.1 Cut-up texts

Level Pre-intermediate and above

Time 20–30 minutes

Aims To highlight the way grammar works across sentences in order to make texts cohesive.

Materials Sets of strips of card or paper: as many sets as there are groups.

Preparation

Find or write a short (maximum 10 sentences) complete text whose sentences are linked in some way. This may be through the use of **linkers** (such as *Therefore, So, However*), through the use of **pronouns** to refer back in the text (as in *The bus was late.* **It** *was also full …*), or substitution, i.e. when a word like *one* or *do* or *did* stands in for a previously mentioned word or **clause**, as in *The bus was full. So I waited for the next* **one**. *I'm glad I* **did**. The linking may also be achieved through the repetition of keywords, or through the use of a **lexical** chain, i.e. a sequence of words that are topically related. Here, for example, is a (very short) text from a children's encyclopedia, in its original form:

Chameleon
Chameleons are African lizards. They can catch insects by shooting out their long tongues. The chameleon can change colour to match its background. It does this as camouflage to protect itself or when it is angry.

(Adrienne Jack. *Pocket Encyclopedia*. Kingfisher, 1983)

Reproduce the text as individual sentences, one sentence per line, each line pasted on to a strip of card, so that the cut-up version of the text looks like this (it helps to number the sentences so that the task can be checked easily later on):

(1) It does this as camouflage to protect itself or when it is angry.

(2) They can catch insects by shooting out their long tongues.

(3) Chameleons are African lizards.

(4) The chameleon can change colour to match its background.

Procedure

1 Write the title of the text on the board (*Chameleons*). Quickly check that the learners know what the title refers to, and allow them a minute or two to brainstorm what they know about the topic. Solicit some ideas from the class, and write up any words that they need to know in order to talk about the topic (for example, *camouflage*). It is important that the learners come to the ordering task that follows well prepared to make sense of the text, since a basic comprehension of the text will be necessary if they are going to be able to put it in order.

2 Hand out the cut-up text, one set per pair or group. Ask them to put it in order.

3 Check the task. It helps if you have a copy of the original text that you can project on to the board.

4 Now, ask learners to tell you what language 'clues' helped them do the ordering task. In the case of the Chameleon text, these might be:
- back-reference using pro**nouns** and **possessive determiners**: *Chameleons* ➔ *They … their; The chameleon* ➔ *It … itself … its*
- agreement of **pronoun** with its **referent**: *Chameleons* (plural) ➔ *They* (plural); *The chameleon* (singular) ➔ *It* (singular);
- **clause** substitution: *can change colour to match its background* ➔ *does this*.

Variation 1

Include a 'rogue' sentence in the mixed-up text, in order to make the task a little more challenging. For example:

Can you put the sentences of this text in order? Note: there is one extra sentence which you don't need to use.

1 The papyrus strips were then pressed under weights.
2 Then someone laid these strips on a frame to form layers.
3 Finally, when the papyrus was dry, a man with a stone rubbed the surface smooth for writing.
4 They not only invented their own alphabet, but they were the first to write on a kind of paper made from papyrus reeds.
5 First people had to cut down the papyrus stems, and cut them into lots of thin strips.
6 This squeezed out the water and squashed the layers together.
7 Papyrus was expensive because it took such a long time to make.

(Extract from *Great Little Encyclopia*. Miles Kelly Publishing Ltd, 2003)

(In this case, the order of the sentences is: 7, 5, 2, 1, 6, 3, and the rogue sentence is number 4.)

Variation 2

To make the task more challenging still, mix together two short texts, the idea being both to separate them and put them in the correct order. For example:

> *Here are two texts that have been mixed up. Can you separate them, and then put each text in order?*
>
> 1 They could buy scented oils and perfumes, read a book or eat a snack!
> 2 Then it was washed and filled with linen to keep its shape.
> 3 Ancient Egyptians were skilled at making mummies.
> 4 Visitors could take part in sports, such as wrestling, do exercises, have a massage or a haircut.
> 5 Roman baths were more than a place to get clean.
> 6 Finally, the body was oiled and wrapped in linen bandages.
> 7 Or they could admire works of art in the bath's own sculpture gallery!
> 8 Next, the body was left to dry for 40 days.
> 9 The body's insides were removed, except for the heart.
> 10 They were also places to relax, meet friends and get fit.
>
> (Extract from *Great Little Encyclopia*. Miles Kelly Publishing Ltd, 2003)

The two texts are: 3, 9, 2, 8, 6; and 5, 10, 4, 1, 7.

Follow-up

Give learners a copy of the text with the **linking** devices removed and ask them to replace them. For example:

> **Chameleon**
> Chameleons are African lizards. _____ can catch insects by shooting out _____ long tongues. The chameleon can change colour to match _____ background. _____ _____ _____ as camouflage to protect _____ or when _____ is angry.

Comments

Note that it is seldom the case that the *only* clues as to the order of the sentences are grammatical. Knowledge of how certain kinds of texts are organized—for example, from the general to the particular—also helps. **Lexical** factors, such a word repetition, also play an important role in binding a text together. Cutting up a text and reordering is an excellent way of drawing attention to these features, assuming, of course, that the text was cohesive in the first place!

3.2 Pronoun shifts

Level Intermediate and above

Time 20–30 minutes

Aims To raise awareness of how pronouns create networks of cross-reference in a text.

Preparation

Choose a story or fairy tale that will be well-known to your students. *Cinderella, Little Red Riding Hood*, or *Jack and the Beanstalk* are possible examples. Use or write a version of it that matches your class's level. Make sure the story includes a number of **pronouns** that refer back in the text. For example, *Once upon a time there was a girl called Cinderella.* ***She*** *lived with* ***her*** *two ugly sisters.* ***They*** *were very cruel to* ***her*** *…*
Make enough copies of the story to go round the class. In order to identify pronouns quickly, it will help if the lines are numbered.

Procedure

1 Tell the class you are going to read them a story. Challenge them to guess the name of the story. Read the text to the learners, but don't mention the name of the main character. For example, *Once upon a time there was a girl … She lived with her two ugly sisters …* After each sentence, pause, and see if anyone can guess the name of the story, or of the main character.

2 At that point, invite the learners to continue the story, orally, either in pairs, groups, or to the whole class.

3 Hand out the printed version of the story, and check any unfamiliar vocabulary.

4 Ask learners to underline all the pronouns in the story, including the **possessives** (*her, their*, etc.).

5 Draw attention to the way many of the pronouns refer back in the text (as in the example in Preparation above). Choose some instances of back-referring pronouns in the text, and invite learners to tell you what each pronoun's **referent** is (i.e. the thing or person referred to by the pronoun).

6 Tell the class that they are going to rewrite the story from different points of view, or in order to take into account changes of character. For example, if the chosen story is 'Cinderella', the task might be to rewrite the story:
- as if *you* were Cinderella;
- as if you were one of the ugly sisters;
- as if Cinderella was a boy (Cinderon);
- as if Cinderella were twins (Cinderella and Cinderon).

Set different pairs or groups different versions of the story to rewrite. Remind them that they will have to pay particular attention to the choice of pronoun.

7 Once learners have written their stories, they can exchange these with other groups and read and comment on them.

Follow-up

Provide a version of the text with the pronouns blanked out, which learners then complete.

3.3 Reference networks—the definite article

Level **Intermediate and above**

Time **20–30 minutes**

Aims **To draw attention to the way persons or things (represented by nouns) become definite (and hence take the definite article *the*) once they are assumed to be part of the writer's and reader's shared knowledge.**

Preparation

Find a text that contains different uses of the definite **article** *the*. Since the word *the* is the most frequent word in English, finding texts with *the* is not a problem! Finding texts whose uses of *the* are easily explained is more problematic, however. The easiest use of *the* to explain is that of 'prior reference', i.e. reference to persons or things that have already been introduced into a story, as in this example (from the beginning of an Arab folktale), where **pronoun** back-references are in *italics*, and **article** back-references are underlined:

> A man who had a monkey wanted to train *it* to weave. But even when the man beat *it*, the monkey refused to learn.
>
> One day the man brought one of his sheep to the loom, and, while the monkey watched, pretended that *he* was trying to teach *it* to weave. The sheep, of course, did nothing but bleat, which made the monkey laugh …

Notice that one instance of the definite article *the* in this text (the *loom*) is not accountable by the 'rule of prior mention'. In this case, *the loom* is definite by association with the idea of *weaving*, which presupposes the use of a loom.

Note also that the text is rich, not only in definite articles, but also in back-referring pronouns, suggesting that the same text can be used to highlight both kinds of referring devices.

Make enough copies of the text to go round the class.

Procedure

Distribute the text and ask learners to underline each instance of *the* + **noun phrase**, and, working in pairs or small groups, to answer this question: *Which noun phrase?* For example:

> … even when the man beat it …
> Q *Which man?*
> A *The man who had a monkey.*
>
> … the man brought one of his sheep to the loom …
> Q *Which loom?*
> A *The loom implied by 'to weave'.*

Example Here is the complete text, with the definite articles explained, according to what the source of the shared knowledge is in each case:

A man who had a monkey wanted to train it to weave. But even when the man[1] beat it, the monkey[2] refused to learn.

One day the man[3] brought one of his sheep to the loom[4], and, while the monkey[5] watched, pretended that he was trying to teach it to weave. The sheep[6], of course, did nothing but bleat, which made the monkey[7] laugh. The man[8] drew out his knife and said to the sheep[9], 'If you do not learn I swear by your young lambs that I shall kill you!' The sheep[10] continued to do nothing but bleat. And then the man[11] did kill it.

At the sight[12] of the blood[13], the monkey[14] jumped into the pit[15] of the loom[16] and began to toss the shuttle[17] to and fro as fast as he could go. Hence the saying[18], 'Kill the sheep[19] and the monkey[20] will learn to weave'.

1 *Which man?* The man who had a monkey (prior reference).
2 *Which monkey?* The monkey owned by the man (prior reference).
3 *Which man?* As 1.
4 *Which loom?* The loom implied by 'to weave' (background knowledge).
5 *Which monkey?* As 2.
6 *Which sheep?* The sheep the man brought to the loom (prior reference).
7 *Which monkey?* As 2.
8 *Which man?* As 1.
9 *Which sheep?* As 6.
10 *Which sheep?* As 6.
11 *Which man?* As 1.
12 *Which sight?* The sight *of the blood* (specification through the use of a post-modifying **phrase**).
13 *Which blood?* The blood implied by *killing by means of a knife* (background knowledge).
14 *Which monkey?* As 2.
15 *Which pit?* The pit *of the loom* (specification through the use of a 'post-modifying' phrase).
16 *Which loom?* The loom that the sheep was brought to (prior reference).
17 *Which shuttle?* The shuttle of the loom: all looms have shuttles (background knowledge).
18 *Which saying?* The saying that follows (forward reference).
19 *Which sheep?* Any member of the class *sheep* (generic reference).
20 *Which monkey?* Any member of the class *monkey* (generic reference).

Comments

The exercise demonstrates the way any instance of the word *the* 'points' in one of three directions: either back in the text, or forward in the text, or 'outside' the text, to the background knowledge that writer and reader (or speaker and listener) both share. Background knowledge includes knowledge of the immediate context (as in *Have you seen the scissors?*), knowledge of the local context (*I'm going to the gym*), and knowledge of the cultural, global—even universal—context (*We watched the sun rise over the Pyramids*).

Follow-up

Learners write their own folktales, or other narrative texts, paying particular attention to their use of articles.

3.4 Sentence insertion

Level Upper-intermediate and above

Time 20–30 minutes

Aims To draw attention to the way grammar and co-text are interdependent.

Preparation

Find, or write, a short text (or texts), one or more sentences of which have been removed from the text and are provided separately. The extracted sentences should be chosen so that their reinsertion into the text depends on recognizing grammatical features of cohesion. These might be: **pronoun** reference; the use of definite articles; the use of **comparative** forms; the use of **tense**—such as the past perfect—to mark time shifts; or the use of the **passive** to maintain the topic of the text in the **subject** position in the sentence. Here, for example, is a paragraph from an academic text, with two sentences extracted. (The sentences have all been numbered, for ease of checking.)

Can you insert these two sentences in the correct place in the text that follows?
A This is how we move.
B The smallest is a bone in the ear, called the stirrup.

Skeleton and muscles

(1) Bones are made of living cells. (2) The largest bone in the body is the femur or thigh-bone. (3) The ribs form a cage to protect the heart and lungs. (4) The skull similarly encloses the soft brain. (5) Where bones meet, they form a joint. (6) Joints are held together by elastic ligaments and soft tissue called cartilage. (7) Muscles are attached to the bones by tendons. (8) When the brain orders muscles to contract, the muscles pull the bones.

Procedure

1 Distribute text and ask learners to read it for gist, before reading it more intensively in order to re-insert the sentences that have been extracted.

2 Check the task in open class, and ask learners to justify their choices by reference to the grammatical features of the sentences and their co-text. In the example text, the extracted Sentence A follows Sentence 8, and uses a pronoun (*this*) to refer back to the whole of the previous sentence. The extracted sentence B comes between sentences 2 and 3 and uses parallel structures (*largest … smallest*) and **ellipsis** (or omission) of the word *bone*, to connect to the previous sentence.

Follow-up

Learners can prepare texts in a similar way for each other, choosing texts from their coursebooks, for example.

Comments

It helps if the texts are in a digital format, so that they can be manipulated using a word processing program. It's much easier to see how a sentence fits into a text when you can physically move it from place to place.

3.5 Sentence insertion—multiple choice

Level Intermediate and above

Time 20–30 minutes

Aims To raise awareness as to how grammar and co-text are interdependent.

Preparation

Prepare an exercise which consists of three-sentence texts. The middle sentence of each text is left blank, and two or more choices are provided for its completion. The choice of sentence should depend on recognizing which organization of information best fits the immediate context.

Example Here is an exercise that targets the use of what are called **cleft sentences.** A cleft sentence is a way of dividing a sentence into two parts so that extra emphasis is given to the information that comes immediately after the main verb (here *be*): for example, *It was Tom who answered the phone. What you should do is learn to drive.* (See Worksheet 3.5.)

Procedure

1 Distribute the exercise to learners. Use the first example in open class to demonstrate how the exercise works.

2 Learners work on the rest of the task in pairs. Allow time for open class feedback, challenging learners to justify their choices.

3 Set learners the task of writing their own texts, based on topics of their choice, incorporating the targeted grammar area.

Worksheet 3.5
Cleft sentences

Choose the best way (*a–d*) of completing each short text:

1 Tom didn't panic, Jack did.
  a *Tom phoned the police.*
  b *The police were phoned by Tom.*
  c *What Tom did was phone the police.*
  d *It was Tom who phoned the police.*
  His quick thinking was praised by his workmates.

2 The security forces were contacted by the committee.
  a *Tom phoned the police.*
  b *The police were phoned by Tom.*
  c *What Tom did was phone the police.*
  d *It was Tom who phoned the police.*
  And the military were sent a fax.

3 Some people think that Jack phoned the police. They are wrong.
  a *Tom phoned the police.*
  b *The police were phoned by Tom.*
  c *What Tom did was phone the police.*
  d *It was Tom who phoned the police.*
  Jack merely lent him his phone.

4 After the initial shock, they leapt into action.
  a *Tom phoned the police.*
  b *The police were phoned by Tom.*
  c *What Tom did was phone the police.*
  d *It was Tom who phoned the police.*
  Meanwhile Jenny started clearing up the mess.

Expected answers to Worksheet 3.5

It is important to note that each of the four sentence choices in the exercise are grammatically correct, but one fits the context more neatly than the others. This is because of the way the information is distributed in the sentence. The best fits are:

1c Tom didn't panic. Jack did. What Tom did was phone the police. His quick thinking was praised by his workmates.

2b The security forces were contacted by the committee. The police were phoned by Tom. And the military were sent a fax.

3d Some people think that Jack phoned the police. They are wrong. It was Tom who phoned the police. Jack merely lent him his phone.

4a After the initial shock, they leapt into action. Tom phoned the police. Meanwhile Jenny started clearing up the mess.

Follow-up

1 Distribute the sentences without their original contexts, and see if learners can reconstruct them.

2 Provide new sentences, using the same structures, for which learners create new contexts, for example:

Jan kissed Kim.
Kim was kissed by Jan.
What Jan did was kiss Kim.
It was Jan who kissed Kim.

3.6 Applying the end-weight principle

Level Intermediate and above

Time 20–30 minutes

Aims To draw attention to how grammar is used to distribute information in sentences so that new information goes at the end of the sentence. (This is called the *end-weight principle*.)

Preparation

Prepare a series of mini-texts that consist of an opening sentence, and a choice of two follow-on sentences. The difference in the follow-on sentences should be that the new information in the sentence is, in one case, in front of the **main verb**, and, in the other case, after the main verb. The preferred choice, according to the **end-weight** principle, is to place new information after the main verb. This is achieved by a number of grammatical devices, including the choice between **passive** and **active** voice, and the use of dummy **subjects**, such as *there*. (See Worksheet 3.6 below which contains six mini-texts, that together form a complete text.) Make one copy of the worksheet for each pair of learners.

Procedure

1 Write the following example on the board:

1 My village square is very pretty.
(a) An old fountain is in the centre.
(b) In the centre there is an old fountain.

Ask learners to say which of the two sentences, (a) or (b) fits best after the first sentence, and why. The expected answer is (b). Explain that in English (as in many languages) it is usual to put new information towards the end of the sentence, i.e. after the main verb. The new information in this case is *an old fountain*. (*The centre* is not new information, since all squares have centres, which is why it is *the* centre, not *a* centre.)

2 Write the following pair of sentences on the board, and ask learners to say which, (c) or (d), makes the best continuation of the text, and why:

(c) The square is surrounded by trees.
(d) Trees surround the square.

Again, according to the same principle, sentence (c) is the better choice, since the new information (*trees*) is placed at the end.

3 Ask learners to identify the grammatical devices that are used, in sentences (b) and (c) to move the new information to the end of the sentence. These are:

- in (b) the use of *There* to fill the empty **subject** slot in front of the **verb**, and the moving of **adverbials** (*in the centre*) to the front of the sentence.
- in (c) the use of the **passive**, to move the **object** of the verb (*the square*) to the subject position.

You should point out that sentences (a) and (d) are not *grammatically* incorrect, but that they don't fit the context so neatly, and hence may sound awkward.

4 Hand out the mini-texts, one copy to each pair of learners. Forewarn them that they will need to justify the choices that they make. Allow time for feedback on the task in open class.

Worksheet 3.6

1 The moon is our nearest neighbour.
  a Deserts and craters cover it.
  b It is covered by deserts and craters.

2 It would be hard to live on the moon.
  a There is no air or water there.
  b No air or water is there.

3 The first person to set foot on the moon was Neil Armstrong.
  a He led the Apollo 11 mission.
  b The Apollo 11 mission was led by him.

4 Armstrong collected rocks from the moon's surface.
  a Scientists all over the world have studied them.
  b They have been studied by scientists all over the world.

5 Armstrong left scientific instruments on the moon.
  a The instruments sent information to the earth.
  b Information was sent to the earth by the instruments.

6 One thing we know for sure.
  a There is no life on the moon.
  b No life is on the moon.

Expected answers to Worksheet 3.6, following the **end-weight** principle are: 1 *b*, 2 *a*, 3 *a*, 4 *b*, 5 *a*, 6 *a*.

Follow-up

Learners should be encouraged to apply the principle of **end-weight** in the writing of their own texts, especially those of a factual or discursive type. One way of doing this is to ask them to identify the given and the new information of each sentence they write, and to check that the latter is placed towards the end of the sentence.

Comments

Although not all the choices in the above text involved a choice between **active** and **passive** constructions, it is a fact that the choice of active or passive is seldom arbitrary, and is often dictated by the end-weight principle. This is why it is important, when teaching the passive, to show how its use is determined by its immediate co-text.

3.7 Exercise 'subversion'

Level Upper-intermediate and above

Time 15–25 minutes

Aims To explore the way grammar choices are determined by the context.

Preparation

Select an exercise from a coursebook, workbook, or grammar study book that requires learners to choose between contrasted (but well formed) sentences, such as one testing knowledge of the difference between different **verb tenses**.

Example In this example, the **present simple** and the present **continuous** are contrasted:

Choose the best way of completing these sentences:

1 'What *do you eat/are you eating*?' 'Chocolate.'
2 Our neighbours *always spend/are always spending* their holidays in Ibiza.
3 I *am liking/like* London, but I wouldn't want to live there.
4 'Where is Dan?' 'He *plays/is playing* computer games.'
5 Amy *takes/is taking* the bus to work every day.
etc.

Procedure

1. Refer the learners to the exercise you have chosen, and ask them to do it quickly, and to compare their answers with a classmate.
2. Solicit answers in open class for the first two or three items, and challenge learners to explain why each answer is correct.
3. Then, ask the learners to think of a context in which the 'incorrect' answer might in fact be more appropriate.

Example For item 1 of the above exercise, the expanded co-text might go like this:

DOCTOR You're very overweight. What do you eat?
PATIENT Chocolate.
DOCTOR Anything else?
PATIENT No. Just chocolate. For breakfast, lunch, and dinner.

4 Ask the learners, working in pairs, to do the same for the other items in the exercise, that is, to try and think of a context in which the 'incorrect' choice would be correct. If this is not possible, ask them to think of what would have to change in the sentences to make it acceptable, while still retaining the 'incorrect' element. For example, for item 3 above:

I *am liking/like* London, but I wouldn't want to live there.

a possible adaptation might be:

I am liking London *more and more*, but I wouldn't want to live *here*.

5 Let learners exchange their new contexts, and comment on their acceptability.

Comments

This activity, in which grammar exercises are 'subverted', is not intended to undermine the authority of coursebooks or grammar study books. It is designed simply to remind learners that, although studying grammar at sentence level is convenient, there are few hard-and-fast rules that cannot be 'broken', once context factors are taken into account. Of course, this only applies to well formed sentences. It would not be possible to find contexts in which each of the following options would be correct, for example:

'What *is/am/are* you eating?' 'Chocolate.'

3.8 Text substitution

Level Pre-intermediate and above

Time 15–25 minutes

Aims To show how grammar and vocabulary choices in one part of a text impact on choices at other parts of the text.

Preparation

Prepare a text that has a number of options at strategic points, the choice of which will determine the choice of option later on. For example, if learners are allowed to choose between the words *Yesterday* or *Tomorrow* at the beginning of a sentence, this will determine the choice of the verb *went* or *going to* later on in the same sentence. Likewise, the choice of the name *Harry* or *Mary* will determine the subsequent choices of **pronoun**. (See Worksheet 3.8 for a sample text.)

Make sufficient copies of the text for each learner, or prepare it as an overhead transparency.

Procedure

1 Hand out the text and ask learners to create their own text, choosing between the items in brackets. Forewarn them that a choice at one point may have a 'knock-on' effect later on. You can demonstrate this using the first sentence of Worksheet 3.8, for which there could be a number of versions.

Example *Dorothy had picked up her child from school, and was taking her to her grandparents' place.*
Dorothy picked up her child from school, and took her to her grandparents' place.
Dorothy had picked up her children from school, and was taking them to their grandparents' place.
Dorothy picked up her children from school, and took them to their grandparents' place.

However, what would not be possible is, for instance:

Dorothy picked up her child from school, and took ***them*** *to* ***their*** *grandparents' place.*

Discuss the possible alternatives with the class, eliciting differences in meaning that are implied by the different options. For example, the difference between *Dorothy took her to her grandparents' place and Dorothy was taking her to her grandparents' place* is significant, in that the former implies they reached their destination, while the latter does not. (This choice has implications, later on, in terms of when exactly the accident happened.)

2 Learners work in pairs or small groups to do the task. They can either delete the rejected options, or write out the text afresh. Early finishers can be set the challenge of producing another, different version of the story.

3 Ask learners to read their completed versions aloud, stopping to comment on, or to check the choices they have made, and to highlight key grammatical distinctions that affect subsequent choices in the text.

Worksheet 3.8

Dorothy [*picked/had picked*] up her [*child/children*] from school, and [*took/was taking*] [*her/them*] to [*her/their*] grandparents' place. She [*was going to leave/left*] [*her/them*] there all afternoon while she went shopping. On the way [*there/back*] [*she/they*] nearly had an accident. It [*was/had been*] raining, and the roads [*were/were still*] wet and slippery. She [*was just turning/had just turned*] a corner, when she saw a dog [*run/running*] across the street in front of her. She [*had just/just*] missed hitting it. It was [*fortunate/unfortunate*] that her [*daughter/daughters*] [*was/wasn't/were/weren't*] there [*because/or*] [*they/she*] [*was/were/would've been*] frightened and [*started/would've started*] crying.

Follow-up

1 Learners can write a completion to the version of the story they have produced.

2 Learners can prepare similar texts for one another.

3.9 Text analysis

Level Advanced

Time 30–40 minutes

Aims To show how grammatical choices are related to choices at the level of textual organization and text function.

Preparation

Choose a selection of texts of a particular text-type. The texts should be authentic and, preferably, short. Their authenticity ensures that they are more representative of their text-type than invented examples. Their brevity means that reading and understanding them doesn't take up a lot of classroom time, leaving time for close analysis of their language and organization. (See Worksheet 3.9a, three texts that are of the type 'embarrassing confessions in a teenage girls' magazine', which I will call *cringe texts*, and which are a regular feature of this type of magazine.)

Make copies of the texts, one for each learner.

Procedure

1 Distribute the texts and ask learners to skim them in order to answer the questions:
- *What kind of texts are they?*
- *Where did they come from, do you think?*
- *What is their purpose?*

In the case of the cringe texts, the answers would be:
- true confessions/embarrassing stories;
- teenage girls' magazines;
- to amuse, entertain.

2 Ask learners to re-read the texts more carefully, for a more detailed understanding, using overall gist questions, such as *What happened to the writer, where, and why? What was the result?* Allow time for silent reading, and pair consultation.

3 Check the answers to these questions, and check any vocabulary items that may be causing learners difficulty. For example (in the cringe texts), the following slang or colloquial items may need to be explained: *fit* (i.e. good-looking), *nan* (i.e. grandmother), *crush* (i.e. person who you are attracted to). Other words or expressions that are important for overall understanding of the different narratives, are (text 1) *slid, gap, got ... stuck*; (text 2) *burned, spit*; (text 3) *boils.*

4 Having checked understanding, ask learners to say what each of the texts has in common, in terms of its overall organization (or *macrostructure*). In the case of the cringe texts, these features might be:
- *an orientation*—the general circumstances of the event, including the setting, purpose, and participants;
- *a recount*—one or more past events leading up to ...

- *the complication*—the embarrassing event, witnessed by a third party (typically an attractive male);
- *evaluation*—how the speaker evaluates the event and its effect on subsequent behaviour.

5 Now, ask the learners to find grammatical features that the texts have in common, for each of the above stages.

Example For the *orientation*, the following features might be considered *generic* (i.e. typical of this particular text-type), based on this (admittedly limited) selection of texts:

- past tense verbs of movement (*went, popped over*);
- purpose expressed either by *for (for a meal)* or *to (to celebrate ... to pick up some stuff)*;
- **prepositional phrases** (in texts 1 and 2): *at the other side of the room, On the table next to us.*

Allow time for learners, working in pairs or small groups, to list one or two grammar features per stage of the macrostructure. Then solicit ideas in open class and write these on the board.

Example With the cringe texts, other generic features might include:

recount

- verbs of mental processes (*realized*) or of perception (*noticed, couldn't keep my eyes off; looked at* ...)
- **past simple** verbs: *sat down; slid; stuffed; looked* ..., etc;
- time **clauses** beginning with *when: When we sat down; When my food came; When I looked at the list* ...

complication

- contrastive **linker** (in texts 1 and 2): *But when I was about to get up ..., But it was so hot;*
- intensifying **adverbs**: *totally stuck; so hot; just paying for it ...;*
- past **continuous** to provide circumstantial information surrounding event: *I was just paying for it; everyone was staring,; The lad was looking over ...;*

evaluation

- negative **verb phrases**: *never go back; couldn't look him in the eye; haven't spoken*
- time **adverbials**: *again; after that; since.*

6 Any one of these features can then become the object of a more extended grammar focus.

7 Sum up by eliciting the generic features of the text-type, both in terms of macrostructure and of specific grammar items. This can be produced in the form of a handout.

Worksheet 3.9a

1 Mind the gap

I went to an Indian restaurant with my family to celebrate my brother's GCSE results. When we sat down, I noticed some really fit boys sitting at the other side of the room. I tried to look cool all night and it seemed to be working. But when I was about to get up to leave, I slid along the bench towards the end of the table—and fell into a gap between two seats. I tried to get up but I'd got totally stuck! The waiters came rushing over to pull me out and everyone was staring. The fit lads were *crying* with laughter. I'll never go back there again!
Sneak's *number one fan, Kent*

(*Sneak*, Issue 82, 2–8 December 2003)

2 Dinner disaster

My family and I went for a meal. On the table next to us was this fit boy. I couldn't keep my eyes off him. When my food came, I was really hungry so I stuffed a huge bit into my mouth. But it was so hot, it burned my tongue and I had to spit it out. The lad was looking over right at that very moment. I couldn't look him in the eye again after that.
Fenella, London.

(*Mizz*, No. 464. February 26–March 11 2003)

3 Gone off the boil

I popped over to the local chemist to pick up some stuff for my nan. When I looked at the list, I realized she wanted me to buy some cream for her boils. I was just paying for it when my crush walked into the shop. How embarrassing? I haven't spoken to him since.
Mizz *fan, Scotland*

(*Mizz*, No. 464. February 26–March 11 2003)

Follow-up

1 Provide another example of the text-type, and ask learners to evaluate how closely it matches the generic description outlined previously. For example, here is another cringe text:

Worksheet 3.9b

4 Pyjama palaver

I went to the supermarket with my dad recently, but I couldn't be bothered to get dressed up properly. So I put my long coat on to cover up my Winnie-the-Pooh PJs. By the time we got to the till, I was feeling really hot, so I took off my jacket. I'd totally forgotten what I was wearing underneath. The shop assistant couldn't stop laughing. I'm never going back there again.

Chloe, London.

(*Mizz*, No. 464. February 26–March 11 2003)

Features shared by this text with texts 1, 2, and 3, include:

- the overall macrostructure;
- similar use of past tense, both simple and continuous;
- time clauses (but introduced by *by the time* rather than by *when*);
- intensifying adverbs: *really, totally*;
- negative verb phrase and time adverbials in the aftermath.

2 Ask learners to write their own cringe texts, incorporating some or all of the generic features that they have identified.

3 Alternatively, ask them to rewrite the text using the conventions of another narrative text-type, for example, a police statement; a film synopsis; or a joke.

Comments

The justification for analysing a single text-type in such detail is that it sensitizes learners to the interdependency of text and grammar in the interpretation and production of *all* text-types. It is also a useful approach for learners who need to master a range of possibly unfamiliar text-types in English, such as those planning to study in English-speaking educational institutions.

Example Short academic texts that lend themselves to this approach include the abstracts for research papers, such as this one (numbers have been added):

Abstract (1) *Amphicoma* (Glaphyridae) beetles are important pollinators of red bowl-shaped flowers in the Mediterranean. The role of color and shape in flower choice is well studied but the roles of inclination, depth, and height have seldom been investigated. (2) Under field conditions, models were used to experimentally manipulate these three characters and visitation rates of beetles were recorded. (3) Models with red horizontal surfaces were visited significantly more often than models with red vertical surfaces. Shallow flower models were visited significantly more than deeper equivalents. Models below or at the height of natural flower populations elicited significantly more landings than models above the height of flowers. (4) Inclination, depth, and height characteristics are all likely to be important components in the flower preferences exhibited by pollinating beetles.

(From *Journal of Insect Behaviour*, 18/1, January 2005)

Even this one example reveals a lot of organizational and grammatical information that might be useful to learners having to read and write this kind of text. At the organizational level, there is a division into (1) background and purpose of study; (2) methodology; (3) summary of results; (4) conclusions. Note that present tenses are associated with sections (1) and (4), and past tenses in the **passive** voice with sections (2) and (3). Note also the use of **comparative** forms in part (3), and **modality** (*likely to be*) in part (4). Note also the presence of long and complex **noun phrases** (for example, *important pollinators of red bowl-shaped flowers; visitation rates of beetles*). A comparison with other abstracts from the same or different disciplines would reveal to the extent that the above features are typical (i.e. generic), or not.

3.10 Text reordering

Level Intermediate and above

Time 20–30 minutes

Aims To sensitize learners to the way grammar is used to sequence events.

Preparation

Prepare a short narrative of five to eight sentences. For example, the following sentences can be used to provide a focus on the past perfect:

(1) Two mountaineers were climbing the Matterhorn.
(2) Their rope broke.
(3) The two climbers fell 200 metres.
(4) One of them managed to phone for help using her mobile phone.
(5) They were rescued by helicopter.

Prepare copies of the text in the form of a handout, or as an overhead transparency.

Procedure

1 Write the following two sentences on the board:

I left home at 8.00.
I arrived at work at 8.30.

Ask learners what changes would be necessary if they were to reverse the order of the sentences. For example:

I arrived at work at 8.30.
I *had left* home at 8.00.

Draw their attention to the way the past perfect is used to clarify the order of events when events are narrated out of sequence.

2 Hand out (or project) the prepared text. Check understanding of any unfamiliar vocabulary. Then, ask the learners to rewrite the text in this order: sentences 5, 1, 2, 3, 4, making any necessary adjustments both to that sentence and to subsequent sentences. For example:

> Two mountaineers were rescued by helicopter. They had been climbing the Matterhorn. Their rope had broken. The two climbers had fallen 200 metres. One of them had managed to phone for help using her mobile phone.

3 Repeat the exercise, this time starting from the third sentence. Continue, suggesting other combinations of sentences, for example:

> 4 → 3 → 1 → 2 → 5
> 3 → 1 → 2 → 4 → 5
> etc.

Alternatively, assign different sequences to different groups.

4 Invite learners to 'polish' the texts, adding **linkers** where appropriate, and incorporating other details (such as *They set out at dawn*), so as to make the text read more like a newspaper report.

5 Comment on the effect that is created by starting with different sentences. Note that when one sentence is placed ahead of the others, the effect is to foreground that sentence, and to relegate the others to the background.

Variation

Turn the task into a race: set a time limit and see which pair or group can produce the most combinations. Check that all the combinations are correct, with regard to the use of tense.

Follow-up

Ask earners to look at authentic newspaper texts, and to note the order in which the events are sequenced. Ask them to identify and explain the verb tenses that have been used in each instance.

3.11 Textualizing

Level Intermediate and above

Time 20–30 minutes

Aims To encourage the use of grammatical devices, including the use of subordination and relative clauses, in order to produce cohesive text.

Preparation

Write a 'detextualized' text, that is, a text that has been stripped down to simple sentences. (For a sample text, see Worksheet 3.11.) Make copies of the text, one per learner.

Procedure

1 Write this pair of sentences on the board:

I ate a sandwich.
I had brought it with me.

Ask learners to make one sentence out of the two, for example, *I ate a sandwich which I had brought with me.*

Write two more sentences on the board:

I peeled an orange.
I ate the orange.

and ask the class to join these sentences and include them in the original sentence, for example, *I ate a sandwich which I had brought with me, and then I peeled an orange and ate it.* Ask the class to identify the different means by which the four sentences have been joined into one, i.e. a relative **clause** (*which I had brought with me*), **conjunctions** (*and*), sequencers (*then*) and **pronouns** (*I ate it*).

2 Distribute the exercise, and ask the learners, working in pairs or small groups, to transform it into a cohesive text of a pre-established number of sentences (for instance, 5 or 6, in the case of the example text above). Point out that they can vary the order in which the information is presented, so long as they retain the general sense of the original. It is useful if the learners write their 'textualized' texts on to overhead transparencies, for later projection.

3 Compare the finished texts, either by having learners exchange their texts, or asking individuals to read the texts aloud, to write them on to the board—or—if the texts have been written on to transparencies, to project them. Comment on the different ways the texts have been 'textualized', suggesting improvements where appropriate, and correcting any errors that may have resulted in the textualizing process.

Example One way of textualizing the text in Worksheet 3.11 might be:

Last week I went to visit my 80-year-old aunt, who suffers from Parkinson's, and has been living in an old people's home out of town for two years. It was raining when I set off and the traffic was slow, so I arrived late. The nurse, who knows me well by now, showed me in, and we stood in the hall chatting, before she took me to meet my aunt, who was sitting with a number of other elderly people, all watching TV. My aunt, who was wearing an Indian shawl I had given her on my last visit, and whose hair had been neatly brushed, looked well. She greeted me warmly and let me lead her out into the garden, where she most likes to sit.
[= 5 sentences]

Worksheet 3.11

Last week I went to visit my aunt. My aunt lives in an old people's home. The old people's home is out of town. She has been living there for two years. She suffers from Parkinson's. She is 80. I set off. It was raining. The traffic was slow. I arrived late. The nurse showed me in. The nurse knows me well by now. We stood in the hall. We chatted. She took me to meet my aunt. My aunt was sitting. She was with a number of other elderly people. They were all watching TV. My aunt was wearing an Indian shawl. I had given it to her on my last visit. Her hair had been neatly brushed. She looked well. She greeted me warmly. She let me lead her out in to the garden. The garden is where she most likes to sit.

Follow-up

Learners can 'detextualize' texts of their own choosing, and exchange these. The textualized versions can then be compared with the original.

3.12 Spoken grammar

Level **Intermediate and above**

Time **20–30 minutes**

Aims **To raise learners' awareness as to some of the differences between the grammar of written and of spoken English.**

Preparation

Prepare two versions of a short dialogue, one of which incorporates features of spoken grammar, while the other is more typical of written grammar. (For an example, see Worksheet 3.12 below.) Make copies of the dialogues, one per learner, or present them on a transparency.

Procedure

1 Distribute (or project) the two dialogues, and ask learners to say what is different about them. It is expected that they will notice the more informal, colloquial nature of the 'spoken grammar' version.

2 Draw learners' attention to these features of spoken grammar:

- **ellipsis** (i.e. omission of words or phrases, particularly **subject pronouns**) as in *Nice bike; Looks like new,* and *Used to cycle a lot;*
- sentence 'heads', as in: ***A friend of mine, his brother*** *… he …*;
- sentence 'tails', as in *one or two months,* ***actually****; Used to cycle a lot,* ***I did****. When I was young,* ***I mean****;*
- **question tags**: *New,* ***is it****?*
- **discourse markers** (indicators of the speaker's intentions): ***Well****, sort of.*

- **fillers**: *A friend of mine, his brother,* ***you know****, he sold it to me;*
- vague language: *sort of; one or two months;*
- 'back-channelling' (to signal interest, understanding, etc.): *Oh yeah? Oh really?*

3 Ask learners to cover up the 'spoken version' of the dialogue, and to reconstruct it, incorporating the above-mentioned features, using the written version as a guide.

Worksheet 3.12

A Nice bike. New, is it?
B Well, sort of. I've had it for one or two months, actually.
A Oh yeah? Looks like new.
B A friend of mine, his brother, you know, he sold it to me.
A Used to cycle a lot, I did. When I was young, I mean.
B Oh really?

A That's a nice bike. Is it new?
B No. I've had it for six weeks.
A It looks like new.
B The brother of a friend of mine sold it to me.
A I used to cycle a lot when I was young.

Variation 1

Record the two dialogues, and play the class the recordings before Stage 1 above.

Variation 2

Cut up the two dialogues into their separate lines, mix the two dialogues together, and paste the lines on to narrow strips of card, so that there are enough sets of cards for each pair or small group. Ask the learners to separate the two dialogues (written and spoken) and to order them. Then continue with stages 2 and 3 above.

Variation 3

Combine Variations 1 and 2: that is, the learners separate and sequence the cut-up dialogues as they listen to the recorded version.

Follow-up

Ask learners to adapt coursebook dialogues so as to incorporate features of spoken grammar. They can then rehearse and 'perform' these dialogues.

Comments

It may be worth pointing out that the features of spoken grammar identified above are not 'inferior' or 'degenerate' in any way, but are simply appropriate to the tenor and mode of the interaction. It is also worth noting that a black-and-white separation between spoken and written grammar is somewhat of a simplification, as many written modes of communication (such as emails and text messages) incorporate many of the features of 'spoken' grammar that have been outlined above.

Appendix

100 most frequent words in English

This list is a guide only, and has been adapted from spoken and written word-frequency lists that are based on the British National Corpus. For convenience, contracted forms such as *'nt*, and *'s* have not been included, and no distinction has been made between the different meanings of individual words such as *like* and *to*. Nevertheless, it should be obvious that the vast majority of the words on the list are **grammar words**. Familiarity with the grammar words of English, and the way they combine with other common words, is fundamental to an understanding of English grammar. It will be helpful to consult this list when planning any of the activities in Part 1: Word Grammar.

1 the
2 of
3 to
4 and
5 a
6 in
7 is
8 that
9 it
10 for
11 was
12 on
13 as
14 with
15 he
16 be
17 I
18 by
19 at
20 you
21 his
22 are
23 from
24 had
25 this
26 but
27 not
28 have
29 which
30 she
31 they
32 or
33 an
34 there
35 her
36 were
37 we
38 their
39 been
40 has
41 will
42 all
43 if
44 would
45 when
46 who
47 said
48 up
49 out
50 can
51 one
52 what
53 about
54 its
55 into
56 him
57 some
58 them
59 other
60 time
61 could
62 no
63 my
64 two
65 do
66 then
67 over
68 than
69 also
70 now
71 so
72 did
73 me
74 only
75 your
76 these
77 any
78 may
79 such
80 people
81 more
82 new
83 should
84 see
85 where
86 first
87 very
88 like
89 just
90 between
91 way
92 years
93 after
94 how
95 our
96 many
97 those
98 being
99 because
100 yeah

Further Reading

Rinvolucri, M. 1984. *Grammar Games.* Cambridge: Cambridge University Press. As its title suggests, a collection of fun activities for practising traditional grammar.

Sinclair, J. (Editor-in-chief) 1990. *Collins COBUILD English Grammar.* London: HarperCollins. An excellent reference grammar for teachers and advanced learners, based on the COBUILD corpus.

Swan, M. 2005a. *Practical English Usage* Third edition. Oxford: Oxford University Press. An indispensable grammar reference book for teachers and advanced learners, organized alphabetically.

Swan, M. 2005b. *Grammar.* Oxford: Oxford University Press (Oxford Introductions to Language Study series). A useful introduction to the subject of grammar, intended for readers new to the formal study of language.

Swan, M. and **C. Walter.** 2001. *The Good Grammar Book.* Oxford: Oxford University Press. The best available grammar reference book for intermediate and advanced learners, with exercises.

Thornbury, S. 1999. *How to Teach Grammar.* London: Longman. A practical book for both new and experienced teachers, aimed at broadening their range of grammar teaching options.

Thornbury, S. 2004. *Natural Grammar.* Oxford: Oxford University Press. A book for intermediate and advanced learners that presents and practises 100 keywords in English, offering a lexical perspective on English grammar.

Thornbury, S. 2005. *Uncovering Grammar.* Second edition. London: Macmillan. This book 'challenges the traditional view of grammar as a "thing" to be learnt, suggesting that it is more like a "process" that emerges'.

Ur, P. 1988. *Grammar Practice Activities.* Cambridge: Cambridge University Press. A book of practice activities that focuses on specific items, mostly of sentence grammar: a classic.

Willis, D. 2003. *Rules, Patterns and Words: Grammar and Lexis in English Language Teaching.* Cambridge: Cambridge University Press. A readable introduction to a view of grammar that links word grammar and sentence grammar.

Useful websites

The Compleat Lexical Tutor
http://www.lextutor.ca/
This site provides a variety of useful programs, including concordancing software and frequency information.

The British National Corpus
http://thetis.bl.uk/
This site provides concordance lines for any word in the British National Corpus (BNC).

Google
http://www.google.com
A useful search engine.

The Independent
http://www.independent.co.uk
A British newspaper's website where past editions can be searched.

Project Gutenberg
http://www.gutenberg.org
A free online collection of book texts.

Glossary

active A **verb** form such as *makes* or *was writing* where the **subject** is the person doing the action, cf. **passive**

adjective A word like *short, red,* or *exciting,* that tells you about the qualities of a person or thing or event.

adverb A word like *slowly, well, there,* or *now,* which tells you about the circumstances of an event, such as how or where or when it happens.

adverbial A word or group of words that functions like an **adverb** and gives you more information about the circumstances of an event. **Adverbials** can be **adverb phrases,** like *very slowly,* or **prepositional phrases**, like *in the corner,* or **noun phrases**, like *yesterday afternoon.*

article The **determiner** *the* (definite article) or *a/an* (indefinite article).

aspect A **verb** form that expresses the speaker's view of the event described by the verb, such as whether it is in progress, or complete. There are two aspects in English: *progressive* (or *continuous*) and *perfect.*

auxiliary verb **Grammar words** like *do, had, was,* etc. that are used with **main verbs**, like *want, play, get up,* etc. to form **tenses**, questions, and negatives.

chunk A combination of words that is more-or-less fixed and functions as a single unit, often with idiomatic meaning, such as *now and again, as a matter of fact, head over heels.* Also known as *lexical chunks* and *formulaic language.*

clause A group of words containing a **verb**, forming the main structure of which sentences are built *[I was working at home], [writing the report [that my boss had asked for], [when the phone rang].*

cleft sentence A way of dividing a sentence into two parts so that extra emphasis is given to the information that comes immediately after the main verb (which in this example is *be*): *It was Tom who answered the phone. What you should do is learn to drive.*

comparative the form of an **adjective** or **adverb** used for making comparisons, such as *older, faster, more comfortable.*

complement A part of a **clause** that gives more information about the **subject**: *She was **a teacher.** You look **tired.*** An **object complement** gives more information about the **object** *She called him **a liar**.*

conditional A sentence containing a **clause** that usually starts with *if*, which tells us about possible or hypothetical situations.

conjunction A word like *and, but, so,* that links two **clauses**, or **phrases**, or words.

content word A word that carries **lexical**, or dictionary meaning. Also called a *lexical word.* cf **grammar word**

continuous Also called *progressive,* one of the **aspects** of English, formed from the **auxiliary verb** *be* and an ***-ing* word**, and typically expressing an activity in progress. For example, *Are you still working? It was raining.*

countable noun A **noun** that has both singular and plural forms, and which can be used with *a/an* and numbers: *a car, three cars.* cf. **uncountable noun**

determiner A word, like *the, some, my, many, no,* etc. that belongs to the class of words that can go at the beginning of a **noun phrase**: ***the** black taxi*; ***my many** friends.*

discourse marker A word like *well, anyway, so, however,* that shows how what follows connects to what has been said or written. *It was not a very good hotel. **Still**, it was cheap.*

ellipsis The omission of words that are obvious from the context: *[We are] Having a wonderful time.*

end-weight The principle by which new or important information is placed towards the end of a sentence.

filler A word or expression, like *erm* or *ah*, that is used by speakers to fill a pause.

grammar word A word that has a mainly grammatical function, such as *it, of, just, any*. Also called a *function word*. cf. **content word**

-ing* word** A word ending in *-ing*, such as *walking* or *seeing*, which is used 1. to form verb **tenses** (*I am* ***walking) where it is also called the **present participle**, and 2. like a **noun** after certain **verbs** and **prepositions**: *I like* ***walking***. *I look forward to* ***seeing*** *you*.

intransitive verb A **verb** that does not take an **object**: *She* ***laughed***. cf. **transitive verb**

irregular verb see **regular verb**

lexical/lexis To do with words, vocabulary.

lexical verb A **verb** that is not an **auxiliary** verb or a **modal** verb, such as *make, understand, arrive*, etc. (Also called a *main verb*.)

linker, linking device A word or words used to link one part of a sentence to another, or to link sentences *Gatsby was rich,* ***therefore*** *popular.* ***What's more,*** *he was good-looking.*

main verb see **lexical verb**

modal verb A verb such as *can, may, should, must*, etc. which is used to express possibility and to make offers, suggestions, commands, etc. Modal verbs function like **auxiliary verbs,** in combination with **main verbs**, to form questions and negatives.

morphology The grammatical system that is concerned with the way words change their forms to express different grammatical meanings, as in *he* ***walks***; *he is* ***walking***.

noun A word like *bus, driver, journey, fare, request*, etc. that can be used after a **determiner** as the **subject** or **object** of a sentence.

noun phrase A word or group of words consisting of at least a noun: or a **pronoun** and which functions like a **noun**: *last night; your old car; I; those big red London buses.*

object A **noun phrase** which refers to what or who is affected by the action described by the **verb**: *I caught* ***the bus.*** *I paid* ***the driver*** (= indirect **object**) ***the fare*** (= direct **object**).

particle An **adverb** or **preposition** which combines with a **verb** to form a **phrasal verb**: *Get* ***up***; *Put your shoes* ***on***; *I looked* ***for*** *the keys*, etc. The **grammar words** *not* and *to* (in infinitive constructions) are sometimes called **particles**.

passive A **verb** form such as *is made* or *was written* where the **subject** is the person or thing that is affected by the action. cf. **active**

past participle A **verb** form that is used to form the **present perfect** and the **passive**, for example, *I have* ***worked***; *The letter was* ***written***. **Regular past participle**s end in *-ed*.

past simple The form of the **verb** that takes an *-ed* ending (for **regular verbs**) and typically expresses past meaning: *Dan* ***called***. *I* ***sent*** *you an email.*

phrase A group of words that form a unit within a **clause**, such as the **noun phrase** *a big red bus* and the **preposition phrase** *at the corner.*

phrasal verb A **verb** and **particle** combination, which often has idiomatic meaning. For example, *I* ***got up*** *at nine*; *Do you* ***take after*** *your Dad?*

possessive One of the **determiner**s such as *my, your, their*, etc. which expresses possession.

possessive pronoun A **pronoun** used to express possession ***Mine*** *is the same as* ***yours***.

preposition A word, or group of words, like *in, on, behind, in front of*, which often indicates place or time, and is always followed by a **noun phrase** ***in*** *the garden,* ***on*** *Sunday,* ***behind*** *the times.*

present continuous See **continuous.**

present participle An **-ing word** that is used to express **verbal** meaning *Jo is* ***sleeping***. *I watched the children* ***playing.***

present perfect The form of the **verb** that combines the **auxiliary verb** *have* with the **past participle**: *I* ***have phoned*** *for a taxi.* ***Has*** *Kim* ***had*** *lunch?*

present simple The form of the **verb** that has no **auxiliary verb**, typically expresses present meaning, and, in the third person singular, takes an -*s* ending: *Jan* ***works*** *in a supermarket.*

pronoun A word like *she, me, it, you*, etc. that can be used in place of a **noun** as **subject** or **object** of a sentence.

proper noun A **noun** which is the name of a person or place or organization, as in ***Sally*** *works for* ***Tesco*** *in* ***Brighton***.

question tag A structure containing an **auxiliary verb** and a **pronoun**, which is added to a sentence to make a question, as in *It's a nice day,* ***isn't it***? *You're not hungry,* ***are you***?

reciprocal verb A **verb** which describes an action in which two people do the same thing to each other *They hugged.*

referent The person or thing referred to by a **pronoun** *Although she was tired,* ***Alice*** *tried to stay awake.*

regular verb A **verb** such as *work, live, start*, whose past **tense** and **past participle** are formed by adding *-(e)d* to the form of the infinitive without *to*: *worked, lived, started.*

Irregular verbs do not follow this rule, for example, *go–went–gone, get–got–got, speak–spoke–spoken.*

relative pronoun A word like *who, which, that,* that is used to introduce a relative **clause**, i.e., a **clause** that gives more information about something mentioned in the main **clause**: *This is the house [**where** Jane Austen lived].*

subject The **noun phrase** that typically comes before the **verb** and tells you who or what is the agent or topic of the **clause**: ***I** caught the bus. **The bus** was crowded.*

subject pronoun The form of a **pronoun** that takes **subject** position, such as *I, she.*

syntax The grammatical system concerned with how words combine to form **clauses** and sentences.

tense The **verb** form which shows whether the speaker is referring to past, present, or future. In English, technically, there are only two tenses: present *(they go)*: and past *(they went).* Future time in English is usually expressed by **modal verbs**, such as *will, going to.*

that-clause A **clause** starting with *that* and often functioning as the **object** of a reporting **verb**: *I was told that the director was in a meeting.* Often the word *that* can be omitted: *I was told the director was in a meeting.*

to-infinitive The form of the **verb** that has no endings, **tense**, person, etc., and which is preceded by *to*: ***To be** or not **to be.***

transitive verb A **verb** that takes an **object** *She **caught** the ball.* cf. **intransitive verb**

uncountable noun A **noun** which cannot be counted, and which therefore has no plural form and does not follow *a/an* or numbers: *some **bread**, a lot of **noise**.*

verb A word or words such as *worked, has, costs, takes off,* that follows the **subject** of a **clause**, and expresses what someone or something does or is.

wh-clause A **clause** beginning with a **relative pronoun**: *I didn't like **what she was wearing.***

yes/no question A question that can be answered with either *yes* or *no.*

Index of grammar items

The numbers refer to the activities where the grammar item is used as an example or where it is mentioned in one of the variations.